Twayne's Theatrical Arts Series

Warren French

EDITOR

Nicolas Roeg

Nicolas Roeg

Nicolas Roeg

NEIL FEINEMAN

BOSTON

Twayne Publishers

1978

Library of Congress Cataloging in Publication Data

Feineman, Neil.
Nicholas Roeg.

(Twayne's theatrical arts series)
Bibliography: p. 146–48
Includes index.
1. Roeg, Nicolas, 1928–
PN1998.A3R63174   791.43'0233'0924   78-5783
ISBN 0-8057-9258-9

Contents

About the Author

I was born one year after Nicolas Roeg started working at Marylebone Studio, entered graduate school the same year *Performance* was released, changed graduate schools and majors (from political science, which I never really liked, to movies, which I have always really loved) the same year *Don't Look Now* came out, and finished my formal schooling just as *The Man Who Fell to Earth* was making its way to the local theaters.

The political science degree (an M.A.) came from Madison, Wisconsin, where I was happy, having just discovered one very special person and movies, all in the same semester, but where I was always cold. The Ph.D. came from the University of Florida in Gainesville, where I lived more than one-third of my life , was happy, and was almost always warm.

While in Gainesville, I developed a taste for Nicolas Roeg, Andy Warhol, and Divine, rock music and houseplants, the ocean and New York in the fall. Also for writing, which has produced one other film book, *Persistence of Vision: The Films of Robert Altman*, a year-and-a-half of film and record reviews for local publications, and several as yet unpublished children's books.

A short while ago, I left family and friends to seek fame and fortune in Southern California. You'll be hearing from me—I hope!

Editor's Foreword

NICOLAS ROEG can hardly be described as a promising young man. He was forty when, after a distinguished career as a cinematographer, he directed his first picture. Since then he has directed only four. None of these has been an outstanding success at the box-office, despite the presence in the casts of such crowd-pleasers as Mick Jagger, Julie Christie, and David Bowie; but all four have become staples on the art theater circuit, especially with film-conscious college students. All seem likely to become classics because of the skillful way that Roeg has brought to life on the screen cryptic, offbeat stories of greater complexity and seriousness than customary film fare.

Nicolas Roeg is, in short, a remarkable example of the film *auteur* who has devoted himself to embodying a unique personal vision in a series of extraordinary creations, rather than grinding out blockbusters to roll up profits for multi-national conglomerates. The surprising, the heartening thing is that so far he has been able to find commercial backing and distribution for his works, for many of our imaginative film experimentalists have been pathetically handicapped by lack of the kind of support that would provide them with the technical resources that they need to realize their projects.

If this series of books has a primary aim, it is to recognize and call attention to the work of creators like Nicolas Roeg, so that their audiences may be expanded and their opportunities to forward their work increased. There are not many people with Roeg's imaginative vision working in the contemporary English-language cinema, and both he and his admirers deserve to be encouraged. This book, we hope, will serve as a stimulus for retrospective programs that will serve to enhance present appreciation of Roeg's artistry and to recruit new sympathizers.

This first full-scale critical study of the director is the work of a young critic who has, as a student of film, grown up with Roeg and who is thus in an enviable position to introduce this lately emerged phenomenon to partisans of established auteurs. With an early, insightful study of Robert Altman already to his credit, Neil Feineman is an unusually articulate spokesman for a generation younger than Roeg that has been principally responsible for the discovery of his work. This writer speaks for his contemporaries with a voice that blends youthful impetuous enthusiasm with a broad and deep knowledge of film that commands the respect of an older audience critical of the superficial hysteria of too many film fans. Feineman has managed—as few have—to master his trades as writer and film scholar without losing the enthusiasm that originally impelled him to want to talk to other people, young and old, about what's worth watching at the movies.

He begins by placing Roeg among the most impressive of his fellow experimentalists in the commercial cinema—Stanley Kubrick, Lindsay Anderson, Ken Russell, and Robert Altman—and he then illustrates how Roeg in his unique works "plays with film grammar" in order to produce films that demand that audiences become actively involved in their imaginative fulfillment—films that are examples of what Feineman calls "experiential cinema."

Roeg's work will never appeal to those who escape to the movies to be passively, mindlessly entertained by ever-increasing violence and benumbing special effects. If film, however, is to establish itself beside such traditional arts as fiction and painting as a "humanity"—an art whose finest specimens enable people to understand something about themselves and others and the universe in which we live, it must also produce what literary critic Stanley Fish has called "self-consuming artifacts"—creations that demand the active participation of the audience in their full realization and that reward such an involved audience with an elevation of their consciousnesses to higher planes of comprehension.

Though Roeg is no beginner in the film industry, his potentially brilliant future remains inscrutable. One hopes that he will be able to continue to make such distinctive, provocative pictures as *Performance*, *Walkabout*, *Don't Look Now*, and *The Man Who Fell to Earth*. But will he? Or will he—like Richard Lester and Brian de Palma, for example—be forced into increasingly sensational projects in order to find the necessary backing? Or will he—like Laurence Olivier and Mike Nichols, for example—be obliged to retreat to more traditional media to find an outlet for projecting his vision? This book accounts for the brilliant first stage of the career of a talented artist whose future may tell us much about the prospects for the artistic growth of the commercial cinema. Our hope is that this first book about Nicolas Roeg will provide some of the impetus that will make others necessary.

Warren French

Preface

THIS BOOK started, I guess, in December 1973 at a dollar matinee at the Carib Theatre in Miami Beach. Because the theater was such an antique, because Julie Christie had my heart ever since *McCabe and Mrs. Miller*, and because it was raining out, I went in. And while I hoped for a decent horror film, I had no idea how good *Don't Look Now* was going to be or how much I was going to be affected.

After getting back to Gainesville and dragging all my friends to see it three or four more times, I still was unable to explain exactly what attracted me to Roeg. His earlier films did not help; it took me several years before I really began to love *Performance* and I have never been able to muster up more than an intellectual tolerance for *Walkabout*. Then, when everyone around me was talking, sleeping, or groaning through *The Man Who Fell to Earth* while I was unable to take my eyes off the screen or my body out of the theatre, I decided it was time to explain to myself and whoever else was interested just what was so important about Roeg; somehow, I never doubted his importance, even though so many of my students and friends did not seem to see it.

At any rate, that is what this book is all about, an attempt to work through my response to the man's films in the hopes of making him more accessible to myself and to you. Many, many people have helped get this book in final form. Russell Merritt, William Childers, Frazier Solsberry, and Kathleen May all gave me desperately needed suggestions and support throughout the year I worked on this. Jim Flavin and company made it much easier by supplying generous technological assistance. Nicolas Roeg made the movies in the first place. Warren French's steady steam of encouragement and friendship helped make this a personal commitment, rather than a professional chore. My parents and sister stopped asking me when I was going to get a real job and never once went for the guilt complex. As usual, Ben Pickard cared about the book as much as I did, willingly giving up hours and hours of his time to read and criticize the numerous drafts of the manuscript. And, once again, Jan endured weeks of my bad humor and messy kitchen tables. To all of you, but especially to Jan, to whom I would again like to dedicate a book, and to those of you I have inadvertently left out, you have my love and my appreciation. And also my apologies for not coming up with a more original way of saying thanks.

Chronology

1928   Nicolas Roeg born.

1947   Begins work at Marylebone Studio, dubbing French films and making tea.

1950   Gets job at MGM's Boreham Wood Studios as a member of camera crew of *The Miniver Story*.

1960   Does second unit work on *Lawrence of Arabia*, especially on the train sequence. Gets film credit.

1961   Is director of photography for the first time with *On Information Received*, directed by Robert Lynn.

1962   Again serves as director of photography for Lynn on *Dr. Crippen*.

1963   Is director of photography for Clive Donner on both *The Caretaker* and *Nothing But the Best* and for Roger Corman on *The Masque of the Red Death*.

1964   Directs photography for *The System*, directed by Michael Winner, and *Every Day's a Holiday*, directed by James Hill.

1966   Is director of photography on Francois Truffaut's *Fahrenheit 451* and on Richard Lester's *A Funny Thing Happened on the Way to the Forum*.

1967   Directs photography for John Schlesinger's *Far from the Madding Crowd* and Richard Lester's *Petulia*.

1968   Begins work with Donald Cammell on *Performance*, his first directorial effort.

1970   *Performance* released.

1971   *Walkabout*, his first solo directorial credit.

1973   *Don't Look Now*.

1976   *The Man Who Fell to Earth*.

1

Nicolas Who?

"WHY," A FILM STUDENT MIGHT ASK his teacher fifty years from now, "did *The Exorcist* gross over 100,000,000 dollars while *Don't Look Now* didn't even make the list of the five hundred top grossing films of the sound era? And why did the same thing happen with *Love Story* and *McCabe and Mrs. Miller?* And with *Star Wars* and *The Man Who Fell to Earth?* Why such big differences between artistic and commercial success?"

The film teacher might well toss his head and smile. "After the French New Wave, British social realism, and the re-Americanization of the film world, artistic advances seem to have given way to trends motivated by economic considerations. Film is, you remember, first and foremost a business. Also, the adjustment to television, still in its primitive stages in those days, made people lazy. So the people were satisfied with the easy, commercial movies Hollywood and the ad-men gave them."

"But," the teacher might continue, "tucked away at the bottoms of the ledgers was a body of films, called by some experiential movies, that were different. Inspired by Méliès, the French surrealists like Clair and Vigo, by Fellini and Antonioni, and by the French New Wave, these film-makers did not want to chain themselves to simple stories about heroes, villains, and a girl, but wanted the freedom to digress from the plot when something else caught their interest or when an intriguing personal fantasy popped up. They wanted their characters to have interesting and dimensional existences, to live, so to speak, rather than just be good, bad, or in service to the narrative. And so that the audience would feel, or would experience the film, instead of merely being passively entertained by it, the directors would forego explanations. To work through the confusion that often accompanied these films, the audiences would have to use their imaginations and directly interact

Roeg on location with David Gumpilil.

15

with the movie. And, because there was just too much in these movies to grasp the first time, the people would have to be willing to see the films more than once. Needless to say, not many were."

"Yes, I understand all that," the student might finally say. "Still, why didn't the people back then realize how good the films were and go to see them?"

Then, things not having changed very much, the teacher might clear his throat, pretend that he did not have time to answer the question, and assign another chapter in the text.

I

To pick the beginning of the modern experiential film becomes a somewhat arbitrary and self-serving task, but *2001: A Space Odyssey* (1968) seems the most logical choice. Visually stunning, in large chunks plotless, and pointedly obscure, *2001* brought in the young drug audience who, while under the influence of the newly fashionable marijuana, gazed happily at the gorgeous images and listened raptly to Richard Strauss's surprisingly appropriate classical music. The disconnectedness of the drug experience lent itself perfectly to the discontinuous narrative that was punctuated with and propelled by the series of "mind-blowing" visual sequences.

Pot-smokers were not the only ones, however, to enjoy *2001*. Many intellectual viewers just loved thinking and talking about what the obelisk meant and why the astronaut had that puzzling experience at the end and what that embryo was anyway. And dedicated film-goers, shell-shocked from television and from the bland, unchallenging commercial films of the time, welcomed *2001* simply because it was new, interesting, and different. Together, this coalition of aging children of the Sixties, intellectuals, and film buffs became the champions of the experiential film, remaining loyal even when the individual directors wavered and "went commercial."

Kubrick, for example, retreated almost immediately from the style his *2001* helped create; *A Clockwork Orange* (1971) featured clearly defined heroes and villains, a fast moving, deliberate narrative, and a predictable, symmetrical structure. Despite Kubrick's defection, however, *2001*'s artistic and commercial success paved the way for directors like Lindsay Anderson, Ken Russell, Robert Altman, and Nicolas Roeg, directors who would deemphasize linear narratives and naturalism in favor of the visual, the surreal, and the non-natural.

Of the four directors, Anderson, the most politically and socially conscious of the group, is the easiest to deal with. After making several industrial documentaries, Anderson turned to feature film. His first, *This Sporting Life* (1963), was a traditional British social realist film, emphasizing class themes, grim industrial backgrounds, and theatrical dialogue and structure. Five years later, however, in Anderson's second feature length film, *If....*, Anderson abandoned naturalism for surrealism. *If....* randomly shifts from color to black and white and back to color again, not as a thematic strategy, Anderson later disclosed, but because his money was running out. Instead of using a flowing narrative, it is organized around chapters, episodes, and events not possible in a naturalistic level of existence. (A boy looks through a telescope, for instance, spies a girl who lives miles away, and watches as the girl smiles and waves to him and, seconds later, appears at his side.) In making his movie, Anderson decided to use the movie's freedom to bend and control time and space; he correctly judged that even though we may be momentarily taken aback by the differences between what happens on screen and what happens in our daily existences, we will see in a new way and understand his comment that revolution is inevitable unless substantive changes are implemented. Although, then, Anderson replaces the stark naturalism of the Social Realists and angry young men with a broader, more surreal style, he has not sacrificed any of his political bite or his ability to communicate.

O Lucky Man, which was finished five years later, in 1973, continues *If....*'s saga and Anderson's fascination with the surreal, the fantastic, and the experiential. In it, Travis, the ex-student-revolutionary from *If . . . .*, begins as a coffee salesman (just as the film's star, Malcolm McDowell did in his own life). Soon, however, Travis becomes a guinea pig, a social climber, a scapegoat, a prisoner, and, finally, a movie star. Believing that success has to do not with any intellectual qualities but with being at the right place at the right time with the right smile, the film destroys a need for conventional motivation or logic. It also feels free to mix the real world with the cinematic one; the musicians, using their real names, record the soundtrack music in front of Anderson's camera and at one point even swoop down to rescue Travis. Actors play from three to four roles; events happen without any preparation or, at times, without any discernible meaning. And the film ends with exuberant documentary footage of *O Lucky Man*'s actual cast party. A seemingly paradoxical combination of political cynicism and irrepressible optimism, the film forces us to enter Anderson's private and Brechtian blend of reality and illusion. Although it looks much different from the mundane realities of our natural lives, *O Lucky Man* is surprisingly able to make its points clearly; because Anderson is so fully in control of his medium, we can appreciate his indictments of society yet feel his joy at being alive and among friends. Most importantly, despite the lack of a conventional plot line that prepares us and explains everything, we are able to accept and respond to the bizarre events on the screen.

Both *If. . . .* and *O Lucky Man* garnered respectable reviews and devoted cult followings. Anderson, however, seems to enjoy working in the theater most—at a lecture at the University of Florida in 1975, he admitted that he did not think that the process of making movies was "fun" and that he felt that he had made a substantial number of films. True to his word, he has not made a movie since *O Lucky Man*, except for *In Celebration*, his 1975 film adaptation of his stage play. Commissioned by the now defunct American Film Theatre, the movie never received commercial distribution in America and is very rarely shown.

That Anderson has not been interested in directing another film is clearly our loss more than it is his. For, even with these few films, *The Oxford Dictionary of Film* considers him to be "more influential than any other single figure in unsettling the complacency of the British film industry."[1]

If not as respectable, Ken Russell has been more prolific, flamboyant, and more committed to the film medium. Although his first feature film, *French Dressing* (1963), introduced the techniques of the television commercial, including the non sequitur, to contemporary feature length films (an introduction normally ascribed to Richard Lester), it is rarely seen or remembered today. Also unseen are the respected television documentaries of famous artists and musicians that gave Russell his early reputation and credibility, while kindly forgotten is his second feature film, *The Billion Dollar Brain* (1967). And although the critics approved of his adaptation of D. H. Lawrence's *The Virgin and the Gypsy* (1970), Russell's real breakthrough came later in that year with his shocking *Women in Love*.

Although in retrospect a wordy and pretentious film, this rococo adaptation of Lawrence's novel seemed in 1970 an unparalleled vis-

ual extravaganza. The infamous candlelit nude wrestling match between Alan Bates and Oliver Reed won breathless adulation from
many and introduced male frontal nudity to mass audiences. Because of her performance, Glenda Jackson won international star-
dom, not to mention an Academy Award. Ken Russell seemed to be
the cinema's brightest new hope.

Russell followed *Women in Love* with the even more striking *The
Music Lovers* (1971). Although more visually adventurous, the film
was much less successful, perhaps because it lacked *Women in
Love*'s narrative movement and literary derivation. It struck many
as being too undisciplined and garish to be appealing; others reacted
to its flagrant and graphic treatment of Tchaikovsky's homosexuality.
It seemed too strange, too perverse, too disconnected; an unpopular
film, it won over few of *Women in Love*'s critics while alienating
many of that film's admirers.

Oblivious to the negative audience response, Russell next made
his most controversial and strongest film, *The Devils* (1971). Again
drawing from a literary source, Huxley's *The Devils of Loudun,*
Russell developed his most dazzling sets and used his most daring
cinematography; his detailed depictions of perverted nuns, sex-ob-
sessed ministers, torture, and burnings at the stake aroused a storm
of criticism and demands that it be censored. It became one of the
few major studio releases to earn and retain an X rating; because it is
so unflinching and so ugly, it remains today one of the decade's most
hated films, despite its considerable body of admirers and its undeniable cinematic flair.

Russell's next film provided an alternative to the increasing un-
pleasantness of his films. Although released later in 1971, *The Boy
Friend* reached many viewers well before *The Devils* because it was
so much safer and thus posed no threats to the reluctant theater
owner. Even though the movie sported Twiggy in her movie debut
and came on the crest of the nostalgia boom, this charming homage
to the Busby Berkeley musicals and to Russell's own visual creativity
failed to become a popular favorite. Most of the viewers seemed to
resent and tire of the unrestrained parade of songs and dances and
failed to get involved with the film's characters, who were uncomplicated caricatures of the old musicals' stereotypes. As with *The
Music Lovers*, Russell's failure to tie himself to a strong, naturalistic
narrative and to more traditional and more conventionally developed characters cost him the mass audience. Even some Russell

fans were beginning to complain; the imagery was beginning to seem a little too ostentatious, vulgar, and calculatedly overwhelming.

Russell jeopardized his career even more with his next film, *Savage Messiah* (1972). Although comparatively quiet and restrained, this biography of Gaudier-Brzeska is a moving and satisfying film. However, perhaps because distributors were afraid of the controversy surrounding *The Devils* and, thus, Russell, perhaps because the Russell fans wanted stronger stuff, and perhaps because the film lacked the stars and excitement necessary to attract a wide audience, *Savage Messiah* was indifferently exhibited and made little impact. Two years later, in 1974, Russell's next movie, *Mahler,* met much the same fate; judged too morbid and too specialized for American audiences, *Mahler* played only the biggest urban markets, occasional film festivals, and university student unions. It had now been three years since *The Devils;* Russell's days as a major filmmaker appeared to be over.

Russell surprised everyone, however, with *Tommy,* which was not just one of 1975's most discussed and debated movies, but also one of the year's biggest commercial successes. Instead of reworking The Who's rock opera into a more coherent and accessible story, Russell opted to make a movie that preserved the spirit and presentation of The Who's musical composition. He spared no expense, building enormous pinball machines, televisions that spewed out baked beans and soap suds, and a degenerate summer camp. Russell took a big risk by not making *Tommy* a more normal movie; after all, his last five films had failed to satisfy large audiences. *Tommy's* subject matter, however, solicited a younger, more receptive audience and lacked the offensiveness of *The Devils* and *The Music Lovers;* it became the surprise hit of 1975 and re-established Russell as a major contemporary force in film.

Whatever advances Russell made with *Tommy,* however, were all but wiped out with his next film, *Lizstomania* (1976). Like *Tommy,* it was a lavish musical lacking in plot and character development. Unlike *Tommy,* though, it had little originality or appeal. The sets, costumes, and episodes were rewarmed, adolescent, and, most importantly, boring. Word of mouth hurt more than the scathing reviews; fortunately for all concerned, it quickly went out of circulation.

Rather than retiring to lick his wounds, as most would do, Russell simply plunged into his newest project, a lavish biography of Rudolph Valentino. For *Valentino,* Russell snared Rudolph Nureyev, who had not been filmed in a dramatic role before. Although it has had a mixed reception, *Valentino* proves that, despite the dismal performance of *Lizstomania,* Russell is still able to get financing and publicity and that, however mercurial, Russell will continue to be a visible force in contemporary cinema, polarizing audiences into violently opposed camps of detractors and fanatical admirers.

What makes Russell so interesting, then (and so much more interesting than most of his films), is his continued refusal to harness his visual imagination into a more refined, more accessible, and more saleable product. Even though a tighter control would probably result in less repetitious, more even, and more effective movies, it would entail an unfortunate and sad compromise on Russell's part. For in the end, Russell's unpredictability and occasional touch of genius make him more valuable, more likeable, and more important than the slew of competent, professional, and cautious directors working today.

Although equally exciting, Robert Altman is a much more controlled and dependable director. After a number of years in television and after several largely unseen feature films, including *Countdown* and *That Cold Day in the Park,* Altman turned M*A*S*H, a movie rejected by sixteen other directors, into the most successful comedy since *Some Like It Hot.* In addition to earning over forty million dollars, M*A*S*H managed to be tremendously innovative for so commercial a movie. There was no real plot, just a series of episodes that had characters coming and going throughout the movie, several people telling jokes at the same time, and a bloody military field operating room as the setting for much of the humor.

After M*A*S*H, Altman's vision darkened somewhat and he lost much of the general public. Even though none of his other films have done nearly as well commercially as M*A*S*H, however, his films have been extremely important artistically and have won him perhaps the most dedicated and influential cult following of any film-maker working in America today. *Brewster McCloud, McCabe and Mrs. Miller, Images, The Long Good-bye, Thieves Like Us, California Split, Nashville, Buffalo Bill and the Indians* (the only one that missed, most people feel), *Three Women* represent what would be an astonishing output for an entire career; Altman has created them all in just seven years. It is indeed a remarkable achievement.

Although of varying appeal, each of these movies shares a need for active and careful audiences. In place of a linearly developed plot, Altman emphasizes characterizations, chance remarks and meetings, curious coincidences, and wonderful little details that are hidden in the corners of the frame. If we do not pay attention, if we refuse to do any of the work, these touches will pass us by.

"You've got to help me," Altman has said. "If you can't help me, my pictures can't be any good."[2] Which is nothing less than a revolutionary attitude because it assumes that the audience is capable of being more than passively and mindlessly entertained. If, he says, we participate in the film, we will have a fuller cinematic experience. If, for instance, we deal with the indistinguishability of reality from fantasy in *Images* (1972), we will be able to experience for ourselves a schizophrenic reaction. If we relax with *McCabe and Mrs. Miller* (1971), we can enjoy perhaps the most beautiful love story of our generation; if we can supply our own histories for the characters in *Nashville* (1975) and round them out ourselves, we become immediately involved with and able to follow the movements of the twenty-four characters and, as a result, will be better able to appreciate the film's events and awesome power. Again, we are expected to use our imaginations, to play our part before we can feel and experience the film. But once we do, we are not likely to be as satisfied with the more traditional, more manipulative, and less challenging commercial film.

Although Nicolas Roeg cannot possibly compete with Altman's output, he shares Altman's talent for making very exciting and artistically adventurous movies. Both are adept at using background music and sounds, brilliant peripheral details and supporting characters, and non-natural and non-rational but emotionally effective incidents. Both strive for and often achieve gut-wrenching editing, breathtaking cinematography, and overwhelming impact. Also, both demand that we use our imagination.

For Roeg, the imagination is so important that it becomes not just a demand on the viewer, but an overt theme in his movies as well. In *Performance* (1970), mind-expanding drugs free Chas's mind so that he can explore the inner, suppressed realms of his personality; in *The Man Who Fell to Earth* (1976), people without imaginations are depicted as empty automata while imagination is seen as the key not to infallibility, but to man's advancement. In *Walkabout* (1971), civilization and the characters suffer because rigid behavior patterns and socialization inhibit the imagination and limit the ability to take advantage of new possibilities. And in *Don't Look Now* (1973), John Baxter is killed because he ignores his imagination and insists on accepting only the rational, the reasonable, the empirical.

For all their similarities, Roeg is a much more difficult director for most people than Altman. Whereas Altman usually has several strong characters to identify with (Brewster, McCabe, Mrs. Miller, Bowie, Keechie, Marlowe, Linnea, Charlie all come to mind), Roeg populates his films with people who are difficult to empathize with. Except for John and Laura, the main characters in *Don't Look Now*, Roeg's most conventional "yarn" picture, Roeg builds his films around bizarre, perverse characters like Chas and Turner in *Performance*, inscrutable aliens like the aborigine and Newton, or essentially unsuccessful people like *Walkabout*'s girl and Mary Lou in *The Man Who Fell to Earth*. As a result, we are asked to identify not with a heroic character, but with Roeg and with the film itself.

Because we are not used to this vantage point, watching a Roeg movie becomes a unique experience. To make it even stranger, Roeg "pushes the structure of film grammar into a different area" by "taking away the crutch of time." As Roeg himself explains, "Some movies will say an event is taking place now, and then, three months later, there is another event. But time is much more instant. I think film is rather like a lifetime that goes in fits and starts. At the end of people's lives, it is difficult to find out what the actual story is. Life is not as simple as 'The Forsyte Saga.' Things happen, time goes by, and nothing happens—then, a crucial moment."[3]

In accordance with this belief, Roeg paces his movies, at least by conventional standards, unevenly. A lot will happen in a short time, will be followed by a stretch where nothing seems to happen beyond some atmospheric excursions, and, then, suddenly, a burst of activity will splash on the screen. Thus, in *Performance*, Chas's browbeating of the lawyer and his dealings with Harry Flowers and Joey Maddocks are crammed into the film's first thirty minutes; as soon as he gets to Turner's, however, the pace is noticeably slowed. As Chas is drawn further into Turner's vortex, Roeg seems to forget that he has a story to tell and concentrates instead on a seemingly directionless accumulation of details. But then, with very little warning, we are hit with the hallucination scene and the film's climactic events, which happen so quickly that we sit in the theater stunned and shaken. In *Don't Look Now*, the first minutes of the film assault us with Christine's death and with the events that will later form the inexorable, intricate pattern that leads to John's death. So that we may feel the process, Roeg stops the relentless, event-filled pace of the first scene and concentrates instead on building an atmosphere of malevolence and impending disaster. Because we are used to an unceasing progression of events in our movies, the feeling that nothing is happening beyond the creation of atmosphere causes many to become frustrated, dissatisfied, and bored with Roeg's films. In a hurry to get to the end of the story, these people stop looking at what is in front of them and feel that the films are pretty but muddled and empty wastes of time.

Because Roeg bends the rules or, as he puts it, "plays with film grammar," he does offend a large number of people. He thus has not, at least in the United States, achieved the audience and acclaim some of his reviews, his talent, his above-the-title stars, or the films themselves would indicate he deserves.

II

Partially because Roeg has received so little attention and partially because his films are so unautobiographical, Roeg's private life and history remain, for the most part, private. What is known comes almost entirely from two interviews, Gordon Gow's in *Films and Filming* (1972) and Tom Milne and Penelope Huston's in *Sight and Sound* (1973).

Roeg told Gow that he had been interested in movies since his schooldays in London. "I'd attempted to run film societies at school, and I always wanted to make films. In the army, I was the unit projectionist. I saw masses of movies."[4]

After getting out of the service, then, the logical thing for Roeg to do was to find a job in the film industry, which was not very hard, considering that his father knew the owner of a film studio. So, in 1947, Roeg was hired by the Marylebone Studio, where he "worked on the De Lane Lea system of putting English dialogue on to French films" and also made the tea (Gow, p. 20). More importantly, he also learned how to edit in the studio's basement.

Several years later, wishing to move upwards, Roeg answered an advertisement for a camera crew job at MGM's Boreham Wood studios. Although bigger and more prestigious than Marylebone, Boreham Wood was still not Hollywood, but "the local factory, inhabited by the milkman's son from Boreham Wood. Local people just went there to work. They got a job and went on to become camera operators beacause, as in any industry, they happened to be there. They weren't passionate about movies" (Gow, p. 20).

Roeg began at Boreham Wood as a clapper boy on *The Miniver Story* (1950) and worked under director of photography Joe Ruttenburg, who had also filmed *Fury* and the original *Mrs. Miniver*. From Ruttenburg, Roeg learned the seemingly obvious but then inspiring lesson that "the only difference between a straight photographer and a cinematographer is that in cinematography, you're dealing with images that create a story" (Gow, p. 20).

Roeg tried to understand and live those words; he "used to take stills and do a lot of work on my own at night, just because I was interested in learning about photography." The set, however, was a different matter; "on the set, I had to make negative tests and hand tests of every single shot. I was even expected to take a hand test box on location, a thing unheard of nowadays. We used to line them up for perfection, rather like trying to become exhibition photographers—but all this was quite unrelated to the idea of images creating the mood for a story" (Gow, p. 20).

He may have been in the movie industry at last, but Roeg was far from satisfied. "When I started out," he recalls, "I wanted to be a movie-maker, and it seemed to me that the way to movie-making was to handle a camera. Then suddenly you realize you are inside a business; and that to make films, you have to have a job. It was all very departmentalized and very like an industry; it *was* an industry."[5]

Because he had movies in him, he envied his friend, Walter Lassally's, gumption. Lassally had also "become impatient with his lot as a clapper boy and was given to wandering around with a light meter in the footsteps of Freddie Young. That was considered an insulting thing for Walter to do," Roeg remembers. "The staff at Boreham Wood thought he was a young upstart . . . getting above himself. He must have been about twenty-four years old. They'd have been quite happy to put themselves in the hands of a surgeon of that age and let him cut their skulls open. But when Walter became a lighting cameraman, some time before I did, I remember thinking how right he was to take advantage of the chance to study the work of somebody like Freddie Young. I'm sure Walter must have felt that he just didn't have enough time to go through the usual routine of working his way up to focus-puller, with the possibility that after five years he might happen to get a break as a second unit camera operator, and perhaps do a couple of insert shots on the floor" (Gow, p. 20).

Despite his admiration of Lassally's spunk, however, Roeg spent the Fifties working on the camera crew, steadily advancing to second unit work, including work on David Lean's *Lawrence of Arabia* (1962). Then, in 1961, he was given his first assignments as director of photography, on Robert Lynn's *On Information Received* and, the year later, on Lynn's *Dr. Crippen*.

There is no record that *On Information Received* ever played in America; it seems equally obscure in England as well. *Dr. Crippen*, which the *New York Times* called "drab," "bloodless," and "pallid," in spite of its documentation of one of the more sensational English crimes of this century, also vanished without a trace.[6]

Roeg's next efforts, however, were more widely seen. His third credit as director of photography was for Clive Donner's low-budget adaptation of Harold Pinter's *The Caretaker* (1963—not to be confused with Hall Bartlett's melodramatic *The Caretakers*, which was also released in 1963). Although the subject matter and theatricality of the film limited its appeal, Roeg's camerwork reportedly made the most of the one room set and contributed to the film's modest critical success.

Somewhat more commercial was *Nothing But the Best*, which was also directed by Donner, also photographed by Roeg, and also released in 1963. A relatively conventional British black comedy, A. H. Weiler in a *New York Times* review described it as "not entirely new but sparkling with gags, wit, and an educated, gratifying irreverence for status and sex."[7] Weiler did not single out the photography in his review; ten years later, however, when Milne and Huston suggested to Roeg that his cinematography made the film look much better than it actually was. Roeg did not argue.

Much more interesting from almost every perspective is Roeg's third offering in 1963, the neglected Roger Corman cult classic, *The Masque of the Red Death*. Shot within Corman's usual three-week schedule, Roeg "loved his attack. He's got a tremendous go to him. He's always doing a dozen different things at the same time . . . . He created a feeling that made you want to really astonish him with good stuff, you know. Hard to define—it's a quality of leadership, I suppose. He says what he wants and it's got to be done, and he makes you somehow want to improve on it. I actually got out of him in rushes one day, 'That's goddam good, Nick.' It seemed to cost him something to get the words out and at the same time he seemed to imply, 'Let's get back on the floor and get on with the rest of it' " (Gow, p. 22).

Critical reaction to the film was astonishing, considering the genre and the condescending attitude most critics and intellectuals have for Corman's films. John Cutts was not atypically overenthusiastic when he called the film "remarkable and beautiful," so "boldly cinematic and full of wonderfully realized effects; I can't remember when I've seen (outside a Minnelli or Cukor film) such a stylized use of color before. Blues, yellows, whites, greens, blacks (notice how red is withheld until the climax)—the film is literally awash in colors. Visually the film is stunning (thanks in no little part to Nicolas Roeg's superb color photography . . .) almost, if not quite, Gothic in its imagery (there's a mind haunting shot . . . of the all-red cowled figure of Death, fingering his tarot cards, crouched by the side of a petrified tree)."[8]

Even the normally staid *New York Times* grudgingly praised the film, primarily because of its visual opulence. "The film is vulgar, naive, and highly amusing," Eugene Archer pontificated. "As for Mr. Corman, he has let his imagination run riot upon a mobile decor scheme. The result may be loud, but it looks like a real movie. On its level, it is astonishingly good."[9]

The Masque of the Red Death proved more than Roeg's introduction to Corman's fast-food approach to movie-making, then. It also gave Roeg his first chance to use color as an organizing principle on which to construct a film. It also gave him the image of the red-cowled executioner, an image he would repeat with much more force in the final scenes of *Don't Look Now*.

Roeg's next two projects, Winner's *The System* and Hill's *Every Day's a Holiday*, were not distributed in America and apparently were met with indifference in England. Although it would no doubt be interesting to see these films to complete any picture we have of Roeg's career as a cinematographer, few have. Fortunately, his subsequent films reached wider audiences.

In 1965, Roeg directed the filming of Richard Lester's *A Funny Thing Happened on the Way to the Forum*. It was a reasonably popular movie, even though the vaudevillian humor at times seemed forced and anti-cinematic. And although the Lester style of quick cutting and disconnectedness attracted most of the critics' attention, Roeg's naturalistic photography helped the movie escape its theatricality as much as anything else. Roeg has made no comment to date about working with Lester. It could not have been too unpleasant, however, for three years later, they teamed up again to do *Petulia*. Also, there is a similar emphasis on shock editing and on fast, jumpy narration in Roeg's work as a director; he may have been directly influenced by Lester. At any rate, *A Funny Thing* was followed by what Roeg considers his most exciting and satisfying cinematographic project, Francois Truffaut's *Fahrenheit 451*.

Roeg was thrilled by working with one of film's masters, as he called Truffaut. "I thought that Truffaut was extraordinary and for the first time in all those years, I felt I didn't mind making movies for someone else." Then Milne asked whether or not Truffaut left Roeg "free on the visual side." Roeg replied, "free inasmuch as . . . no. We'd discussed the style before it started and I said I thought it should look like Toyland; and he said, 'That's exactly what I've been interested in. It should be like a Doris Day picture.' We did a couple of tests, he liked the visual style, and he left me pretty well free on that. But the precision of the film, the actual set-up of the film, that was his. It was totally his film. We would offer things, obviously; when you like someone and you really admire their work, you can't help beginning to tune your mind to theirs" (Milne, p. 6).

Despite Roeg's admiration of Truffaut and of *Fahrenheit 451*, it was not particularly well-received because it was thought too plodding, literary, and contrived to be really effective. Roeg, however, thought the film "perfect" and ahead of its audience (Milne, p. 5). To this day, Roeg feels that the film strongly influenced him; although he has never been more specific, his ideas of stylized, deliberate, and even cold films were almost certainly strengthened by his experience in Toyland.

Rather than pursuing the directions suggested by *Fahrenheit 451*, however, Roeg found himself working within the romantic, more traditionally picturesque style of John Schlesinger's *Far From the Madding Crowd*. It was less of a popular and critical success than *Fahrenheit 451*; but like it, *Far from the Madding Crowd* is most remembered for its look, or its cinematography. According to Roeg, there is a further similarity between the two films; both were mis-understood by and at odds with an inflexible audience (Gow, p. 21).

Roeg and Schlesinger were eager, Roeg claims, to "get the very feel of Hardy's countryside on to the screen. I think the film was underestimated. It came at a time of change. John tried to capture the feeling of the seasons through a rather leisurely pace—and it came at a time when cinema audiences were accustomed to another sort of pace. They weren't ready for a film that virtually said, 'Wait a minute—there's also time to sit back and relax and watch, and just be involved in the unfolding of a tale,' because they simply hadn't been seeing that kind of film for some time. Maybe ten years before they'd have accepted it. But they'd gotten used to something faster. I think if people saw *Far From the Madding Crowd* again now, they would appreciate it much more" (Gow, p. 21).

Maybe so; one thing, though, is certain. When the film was ini-tially released, it was panned, called "sluggish, indecisive, banal, uninvolving." In fact, the only aspect of the movie to win praise consistently was Roeg's cinematography. Bosley Crowther's re-marks are typical: "he has given much of his picture to brilliant color illustrations of the lovely countryside. . . . Indeed, the environment is more impressive than the slow, mawkish drama it con-tains . . . .(it has) rather handsome and slightly self-conscious photography."[10]

Roeg's reputation as a cinematographer continued to prosper in-dependently of the commercial and even critical fate of the films he worked on. His final assignment as director of photography, Lester's cult film, *Petulia* (1968), proved no exception. Although the photog-raphy had a small, vocal group of admirers, the film belongs more to Lester and his obtrusive editing and almost random plot develop-ment than to Roeg's beautiful but functional photography. And al-though Roeg's later disconnected editing may seem reminiscent of Lester's, *Petulia*, like the other films, forced Roeg to adapt his per-sonal work to the director's overall concept, which, in the end, he maintains, "isn't difficult to do, provided you get on well with a director and admire his way of doing things" (Gow, p. 21).

Still, such compromises take their toll. As Roeg explains, the cameraman cannot help but influence a film. "Being a cameraman in motion pictures is the most extraordinary job because it's nearly at the final decision. Nearly. And over-influence can shatter a director

to pieces, can destroy what he's doing. . . . It's a matter of diplo-
macy, really, because if you become too strong with what might be a
weak man but a brilliant director, that's wrong. But yes, you can feel
you're influencing a film, and if you feel you're influencing it to the
point that you've got everything out of the man's mind there is to
get, then. . . ." (Milne, p. 6).

Ultimately, however, the film still belongs to the director. And
since today's film industry is not as stratified now as it was when
Roeg began and since the prevailing attitude now is, as Roeg says,
"Do it! It doesn't matter whether you know anything about it or
not," Roeg decided to be a director and began looking for financing
for his first directorial effort, *Walkabout* (Milne, p. 5).

Roeg had read James Vance Marshall's novel, *Walkabout*, right
after he finished *Petulia*, had been attracted to the story and to the
Australian locale (which he was familiar with from his second unit
work on Fred Zinnemann's 1960 *The Sundowners*), and convinced
National General to back the film. He then talked English play-
wright Edward Bond into doing the screenplay, which he thought
should be about a journey. Roeg then left Bond in Cambridge to
write while he went to Australia, where he spent eight weeks "going
everywhere" (Milne, p. 6). When he returned from Australia, he
"rushed up to Cambridge and asked how it was going. Rather
diffidently [Bond] said, 'I think it's rather good' and he handed me
just fourteen pages of handwritten notes. They were *exactly* what I
wanted" (Milne, p. 6).

Unfortunately, they were not at all what National General
wanted; after reading them, the company decided to pull out of the
film. But, luckily, at about this time, Donald Cammell wandered
back into Roeg's life.

As Roeg explains it, "Donald and I had had a kind of running
relationship for years, drifting apart and coming together
again . . . .we'd had different backgrounds, inasmuch as Donald
had been a painter and then relatively recently a screenwriter (who
had just done 1968's *Duffy*), and I had been a cameraman . . . . I'd
been stuck at a point where the reaction was, 'Oh well, he couldn't
do it because he's a cameraman.' Similarly, Donald was stuck with
being a painter. So we had to make a leap; and we were perfect for
each other, we could build on each other" (Milne, p. 5).

A script came from Cammell, "just a few pages that Donald had
written—a notion for a film about a gangster in London's under-

world, and the relation of that specific kind of violence to the violence in human nature." Money, however, was not forthcoming because of that script, but rather on "the strength of Mick Jagger's decision to accept the role of Turner" (Gow, p. 22). And once he did, the show was on.

As Roeg remembers it,

Performance was a curious film in that we went on the floor and the construction came after. That's why Donald and I never separate our contributions. It became like our lives. We went on the floor with an outline, an idea, and about the first three scenes; there wasn't a script; and then two of us were doing all the jobs of writer, director, cameraman; it was perfect. We got together in a mysterious way, just worked night and day, day and night, and it began to live. When we went on the floor each day, though, the scenes were exact; we knew the intention, and the artists knew the intention, so they had an influence in a subjective rather than objective way, insofar as their behaviour patterns would take shape. But the secret of the film, I mean the secret inside the film, was totally locked between Donald and myself. I don't think anyone at any stage during the shooting really knew that little secret. . . . Sandy Lieberson, the producer, had incredible faith; he liked the movie as it was going. But there never was a final script, and it was a marvelous stroke when Warner Brothers flew a man over to stop the film because we weren't sticking to the script. Show us where we're straying, we said. "Well," he said, "I haven't got a copy here, but they tell me. . . ." (Milne, p. 8)

Yes, yes indeed.

Warner Brothers' headaches were not over, though, when filming was completed. In fact, it must have seemed as if they were just beginning. The problem was that company executives on both sides of the Atlantic simply did not know what to make of the film or what to do with it. Not only was it impossible to understand, but it seemed to be advocating hallucinatory drugs and homosexual behavior. Even if this was 1970, the heyday of the counterculture and the dawn of the Aquarian Age and acceptable weirdness, some things still seemed, well, a bit much.[11] And had someone other than Mick Jagger, the lead singer of the Rolling Stones and a potential drawing factor at the box office, been the star of the film, it might never have been released. Because he was, however, financial considerations edged out the moral and aesthetic hesitation of the executives and *Performance* made its way into the theaters.

As soon as it opened, the movie divided critics, some of whom felt it the most challenging, innovative, and powerful film of recent years, while others felt it the most convoluted, pretentious, and offensive. Regardless of the intellectual controversy, Jagger did not demonstrate the expected box office appeal; the film's subject matter and style proved too much for all but the most urban audiences. *Variety* records it as being in general release for less than eight weeks, playing in four to nine cities and in one theater in each city (with the exception of one week where it played in sixteen showcase theaters). Before it vanished from the list of top grossing films, it amassed only $581,248.[12]

Despite such a poor box office record, *Performance* quickly attracted a devoted following and was the subject of numerous essays and arguments. Throughout the years, its reputation has grown; six years after its first release, for instance, it was the subject of Larry Gross's "Film Après Noir" article in the July-August 1976 *Film Comment*. And in the summer of 1977, the film was re-released in London. Not only were the reviews more uniformly positive, but attendance surpassed initial expectations and the film's run was extended by several weeks.

No such controversy accompanied the release of *Walkabout*, which also opened slowly in a small number of theaters. When it was reviewed at all, the film usually received favorable comment. There seemed, however, to be a marketing problem. Twentieth-Century-Fox seemed to approach it as a children's film, but since it lacked a Walt Disney formula, its ability to attract a large audience appeared doubtful. So instead, the film was handled as a "class" art film for the entire family. It played in the summer of 1971 for five weeks in a small New York theater; rather than an audience developing, however, attendance dwindled each week. Through the fall of 1971, it played one or two week runs in various cities; by late October, when it drifted out of release, it had returned only $633,000 in film rentals.[13]

Like *Performance*, however, *Walkabout*'s financial record is misleading. For while it never became a success in the commercial houses, *Walkabout* is widely shown in revival houses, on college film programs, and, most surprisingly, in churches and schools. These groups have been unexpectedly untroubled by the film's nudity and pleased by children's enthusiastic response to the film. So, even though the movie never became a blockbuster, it has found its audience and continues to be shown regularly, five years after its release. It may not be rich, but it is happy.

Unlike *Walkabout, Don't Look Now*'s reputation preceded the film's opening. The reputation had little to do with the movie's occult subject matter or its glowing reviews, but stemmed instead from its love scene. Gossip columnists had a field day with reports of the steamy, authentic, explicit sex scene between two major stars, Julie Christie and Donald Sutherland. To most people's regret, however, the scene was cut for American audiences so that an X rating could be avoided (although, people who have seen both reassure us, the difference is minimal, possibly not even noticeable). So, despite reviews like "the most subtle and sophisticated horror film ever made," "surpasses even Hitchcock," and "a dark and frightening experience unlike anything ever filmed," what most people wanted to know was whether or not Julie and Donald were "really doing it."[14] (Even today the love scene excites and titillates; *Time* magazine reported in a story about private screenings of films in Hollywood that the most requested print was a series of outtakes from *Don't Look Now*'s love scene.)

Despite the publicity surrounding the scene and the excellent reviews, *Don't Look Now* never really took off at the box office. The average viewer seemed to be put off by the loose ends, the reliance on atmosphere, and the ugliness of the death scenes; although it was Roeg's most commercial film, sporting a relatively lucid plot, two stars, an exotic locale, and a Christmas release date, the film proved too strange, unsettling, and confusing for a mass audience. Pauline Kael's reaction explains the film's failure to become widely popular; she left "still seeing shock cuts and feeling slightly disassociated . . . . ten minutes or so passed before it [the environment] assembled itself and lost that trace of hostile objectivity."[15] Devoid of the camp humor and reassuring ending of most horror films, *Don't Look Now* pushed us too close to the abyss; to a lot of people the solution was not to look or, since they already had gone to see it, at least to encourage their friends not to see it.

As a result of poor word of mouth and unaggresive distribution, *Don't Look Now* concluded its first and last general release with film rentals in this country of $1,283,516.[16] And while this may sound like a lot of money, it is a paltry sum when compared to grosses of the big hits or even of some modest successes. True to Stephen Farber's prediction, though, and consistent with the earlier two

Roeg films, *Don't Look Now* did not go away but "keeps turning up in underground film programs and classic revival series."[17] Among fans, it has taken its place alongside *The Invasion of the Body Snatchers, Psycho,* and *The Night of the Living Dead* as one of the truly great horror films of all time, capable of frightening us no matter how many times we have seen it or how sunny it is outside when we leave the theater.

Three years after *Don't Look Now,* Roeg completed his most eagerly awaited film, *The Man Who Fell to Earth.* Although it did surprisingly well in its first release, earning just under four million dollars from American theater rentals between June and October of 1976, only a few confessed to being really excited by the film.[18] Nigel Andrews summed up the prevailing opinion best: "it contains enough ideas for six different films, and far too many, in my opinion, for one."[19] This proliferation of ideas and the film's lack of a visual or intellectual structure that would have enforced a coherence alienated, then, much of the film community; Roeg's refusal to make a story about "little green men and lots of dials and apparatuses" irritated the science fiction crowd. There was not much audience left.

One of those alienated from the film was its American distributor, Walter Rugoff. (One of the most unusual things about *The Man Who Fell to Earth* was that, although shot in America, the film was financed completely by British investors.)

According to Mel Gussow's account in the *New York Times,* Rugoff held a screening of the film at Dartmouth; when only fifty per cent of the students there said that they would recommend the film to a friend, Rugoff became upset. So upset, in fact, that he hired not just a new editor, but also Richard Simons, a member of the Department of Psychiatry at the University of Colorado Medical Center. Although some questioned the morality of hiring a psychiatrist to doctor up the film, Rugoff claims he just wanted advice. And Simons felt he was acting within "the context of someone who loves film and knows something about Roeg's work." Simons, incidentally, was especially partial to *Walkabout.*

In the end, Rugoff ordered four cuts. One eliminated some of Bryce's sexual exploits and another removed a scene showing Bryce in a Santa Claus costume (an allusion to *Don't Look Now* perhaps?). Also lost was a scene of a terrified Mary Lou uncontrollably urinating after seeing Newton without his earth costume, along with a scene in the incarceration sequence that shows Newton threaten Mary Lou with a revolver and then make love to her. (This last scene was supposed to feed into and amplify the ping pong scene.)

When asked to justify the cuts, Simons explained that in the final segment of the film "I felt the whole thing began to deteriorate. I couldn't grasp where it was going . . . . I thought it was a disaster." The cuts, which eliminated Newton's harshest, most objectionable actions, were supposed to make Newton more sympathetic and less jaded as a character and thus provide the movie with a new focus and direction.

But not only did the cuts fail to provide this focus for most people; they also meant that Rugoff and Simons had taken Roeg's work away from him and, against Roeg's wishes, had mutilated it. Rather than understand and accept Rugoff's actions, Roeg felt "totally distressed and upset," claiming that they had substantially altered the film. The scene with the gun, Roeg claimed, was especially necessary because he wanted to show how Newton and Mary Lou had aged and how Newton had become "totally human." In other words, Roeg wanted Newton to appear less sympathetic and more jaded; by whitewashing his character so as to arouse our identification with the character, the cuts weaken and change the intent of the film.

Although justifiably angry over the cuts, Roeg seems resigned to them, being no stranger to having his movies shortened by the producer or distributor. He does not believe, however, that the cuts have been made for the stated reasons, be they censorship, cultural differences from one society to the other, or economics. Instead, he attributes them to his efforts at pushing the "structure of film grammar into a different area . . . . Whenever one plays with film grammar, it offends people."[20] If Roeg is right, if he does offend people, it is only because we seem instinctively and ridiculously to fight change. For, as we shall see, Roeg is giving us a chance to look at some beautiful, challenging, and different movies. To me, that seems more a cause for celebration than for offense.

2

Performance

" 'IT WAS CLEAR that this film, for whatever the reasons, was having a tremendous emotional effect on people intimately concerned with it which couldn't be countered or contained by rational argument,' said Lieberson [*Performance*'s producer]; 'It was to have the same effect on nearly everyone who saw it. It changed people from relatively reasonable individuals into impassioned denouncers of the evil they claimed it represented. We really began to wonder had we made such a corrupt film. It was a nightmare,' " wrote Alexander Walker in *Hollywood U.K.*

* * *

"*Performance* was the film in which Jagger put the make-up on—and hasn't taken it off since," runs a legendary rock quote from *Creem* magazine.

* * *

"The aftermath of *Performance* was even stranger in the case of James Fox. He retired from the world that had made him a star. Barely a year after its screening, and despite lucrative offers from film producers, he abruptly gave up the world of movie-making and announced his conversion to evangelical good works as a member of a sect called the Navigators. At the time of writing [1975], he is still actively engaged in this vocational work, preaching the Gospel and seeking converts for Christ in the midlands of England," Walker continued.[1]

* * *

"*Performance*—Substandard crime meller with sadism and sex hypes. Dull b.o. outlook. For the psyched set," said *Variety*'s review.[2]

* * *

(*Performance* was co-directed by Roeg and Donald Cammell. As Roeg himself has said, "it's impossible to sort out the elements in *Performance;* it's a fifty-fifty collaboration and an extraordinary event in both our lives at the time."[3] As a result, it is also impossible

really to talk about *Performance* as being Roeg's movie. Since, however, this book is about Roeg and because it is a tremendous stylistic
convenience, I shall refer to *Performance* as Roeg's. Please remember, however, that Roeg co-directed the film with Cammell,
who at all times deserves half the credit—or blame.)

Many directors struggle through years of movies before achieving
a discernible film style. Not so with Nicolas Roeg; in his first film,
Performance, he flaunts the visual extravagance, intellectual complexity, and anti-naturalism that will become his trademarks. The
film also announces Roeg's disregard for conventional plots and
characters and his penchant for episodic, atmospheric movies. And
most of all, it invited us to enter Roeg's personal world of confusion
and madness.

On its most mundane level, *Performance* is the story of a gangster, Chas, who is on the run. Chas works for Harry Flowers, a
powerful British mobster, and enjoys his work. Because he likes
being a gangster and because he plays his role so well, Chas loses his
objectivity and disobeys Harry by shaking down his ex-best friend,
Joey Maddox. Chas's disobedience angers Harry, who believes in a
strict separation between business and personal matters and in an
even stricter adherence to the organization's chain of command.
Because Chas performs as a loner and not as a "cog" in the organization, Harry and Denny, Harry's business manager, feel that Chas is
an "out of date" man.

Shortly thereafter, Chas kills Joey. Terrified by the resulting
publicity from the gangland murder and the possible legal ramifica-
tions, Harry decides to have Chas killed, rather than help him
escape. But because Chas understands the ways of the organization,
Chas realizes Harry will try to have him killed. So, with the aid of
Tony, his close friend, he tries to flee from England. While the
escape is being planned, Chas hides at a house owned by Turner, a
paranoid, bizarre ex-rock star who lives in his strange, psychedelic
house with two women. Although Turner thinks that Chas is a
"washed up cabaret artiste" who is not good enough for his "beautiful basement," Chas convinces Turner to let him stay. Chas, it
seems, offers an attractive alternative to Turner, who has become
bored and "stuck in his old image."

Through drugs and through an increasingly erotic attraction to
Turner, Chas is drawn deeper and deeper into Turner's world. Chas

dons wigs, make-up, and women's clothing, experiences music as
Turner and other musicians do, and becomes comfortable in his
dealings with "weird" people. In addition, through a discussion with
Turner's secretary, a woman named Pherber, he realizes that he has
been suppressing the female side of himself and has been operating
in only a limited sphere of his potential.

After an enlightening drug experience, Chas is reminded by
Turner that he has to call his "agent," Tony. In the ensuing telephone conversation, which is monitored by Flowers' gang, Turner
reveals the address of his house (and of Chas's hideaway). The
gangsters come to Turner's house; as soon as he sees them, Chas
goes to Turner's bedroom. Turner tells Chas that he needs to talk
some more, that he knows where Chas is going, and that he wants to
come along. As if in answer, Chas shoots and kills Turner and is then
escorted to Harry's car. As the car moves past the camera, however,
Turner's face, not Chas's, stares out of the window at us.

Without that final glimpse of Turner's face in the car, *Performance*
would be a complicated but less elusive tale of a gangster who has
become an anachronism, a sort of psychedelic *Wild Bunch*. The
similarities are, after all, there. Chas's inability to adapt to the more
respectable, more corporate nature of modern crime makes him a
dangerous liability, one that must be eliminated.

Chas is not just an old fashioned gangster, but an old fashioned
person. Before he goes underground, he takes the time to call his
mother; he tells Tony that he is disgusted by all the "long hair,
beatniks, druggies, free love, and foreigners" at Turner's "freak
show." Alienated from both the business and social worlds of contemporary England, he thinks of himself as "The Lone Ranger,"
isolated from the rest of the people he comes in contact with. And
dependent on them as well: for all his perceptions of being alone, he
realizes that Harry and Turner control the "buttons" that determine
whether he will live or die.

Once inside Turner's "garden," Chas is forced to examine his
values more closely. Through the use of drugs and the support of
Turner, Pherber, and Lucy, the other woman living at the house,
Chas realizes that he has repressed many facets of himself and experiments with changing his image. Soon Chas becomes more
comfortable with his new costumes and more trusting of Turner. In
the end, however, perhaps because Turner betrayed Chas by

revealing Chas's whereabouts, Chas kills Turner. Thus, despite Turner's considerable appeal to Chas, Chas reverts to his role as the Lone Ranger and old-fashioned executioner.

The movie does not, however, stop with Turner's death; it continues until we see Turner's face looking out the car window. That shot, especially when considered along with all the other hints about transformations, images, and performances, indicates that *Performance* is much more than a story about a gangster's death. In the final moments of the film, Chas has on some level become Turner, or Turner has become Chas; whatever, the identity transference, no matter how confusing, startling, and ambiguous, becomes the film's key issue.

However unexpected the ending may seem, Roeg has both visually and verbally prepared us for it from the beginning of the film. In the first sequence of the movie, for example, Chas's lover looks into a mirror and applies a red dot to her cheek. Shortly thereafter, the narcissistic Chas looks into the mirror and touches his cheek on the same spot, presumably wondering what he would look like with that red dot on his cheek.

The lawyer's speech, which immediately follows, is more obvious and more explicit. Declaring that the age of the small, individual businessman is over, he makes a semantic but realistically worthless distinction between "merger, a perfectly legitimate merger" and a "takeover." "I say merger, not takeover," he says. "Words still have meaning, even in this age of the computer." As the lawyer talks, the noises of unseen computers obscure his words as Roeg cuts to a scene of Chas throwing a recalcitrant client's office machine through windows and punching the client in the stomach. Roeg then cuts back to the jury, intently listening to the lawyer. In a series of jump cuts, the jury gets smaller and smaller; as they are about to recede into the background, we realize that they have become patrons of a sordid pornographic movie house. After Chas roughs up the theatre owner for not paying his bills, he goes to Harry's office where he learns that Joey has refused an offer to join the mob and is in need of a "little nudge." The meaning of the lawyer's and Harry's speeches should now be clear; the person taking over considers the process a merger, while the person who is taken over knows that the word "merger" is a euphemism. And the jury's transformation into an audience indicates that the merger/takeover does not just apply to business organizations, but that it can happen to people too.

Turner's first appearances in the film subliminally reinforce the concept of identity transferrence. When Joey and his henchmen splash red paint on the walls of Chas's apartment, we see Turner's arm (although we do not yet know it is Turner) spray-painting his red wall black. He is, it turns out, painting a black "T" on the wall, suggesting Turner's future ownership of or at least association with Chas. When Joey's sidekick sees Chas shoot Joey, he sees the back of Turner's head, not Chas's. When Chas dyes his hair red, we again see Turner, still painting his red wall. And when Chas washes the red out of his hair, he notices and stares at a poster on Turner's bathroom wall, a poster that accentuates Turner's red hair and lips. Although we lack the information to intellectually evaluate these incidents, they visually prepare us for the relationship between Chas and Turner.

At least in the early part of the film, neither Chas nor we in the audience have much interest in or trouble with the concept of identity. When people ask Chas who he is, he replies that he knows who he is. Harry, for example, asks him, "Who do you think you are, the Lone Ranger?" Chas's answer is, "I know who I am, Harry." Later, when Chas is trying to convince Turner to let him stay, Chas says that he is "determined to fit in here," that, as an artist, he needs this "bohemian atmosphere," "I'm an artist, Mr. T. Like yourself," he says. Turner, though, is still reluctant. "I wonder," Turner asks Chas, "If you were me, what would you do?" "I don't know," Chas answers back, "It depends. It depends who you are. Which I don't know." "Who I am?" Turner says. "Do you know who you are? Harry?" "Yes," Chas answers. And because Chas knows who he is, Turner decides. "Well," he says, "that simplifies that. You can stay. On a daily basis."

Although we do not yet know why Turner would refer to Harry, we can see that Turner lets Chas stay only because Chas is so sure of his identity. Turner knows from the beginning that Chas is not a juggler, but is hiding from something or someone. But because Chas is so secure in his image, because he is so certain of who he is, Turner, for reasons we cannot yet know, decides to let Chas live in his house.

As soon as Chas moves in, however, Turner and Pherber begin undermining that security. After giving Chas a psychedelic mushroom, Pherber takes Chas to bed. While in bed, she places a mirror in front of one of Chas's breasts so that his chest becomes a compo-

TOP: Chas "the bullet" after killing Joey Maddocks.
BOTTOM: Pherber gets inside Chas.

site of one of his breasts and (the reflection of) one of her's—half-man, half-woman. Next, Pherber places the mirror in front of her face so that his face is transposed onto her body. Finally, she puts the mirror in front of his face, making her face appear as part of his body.

"Did you ever have a female feel?" she asks him as she plays with the mirror.

"No, never. I feel like a man, a man all the time," asserts Chas, who is most upset by Pherber's visual and verbal games.

"That's awful, that's what's wrong with you, isn't it?" Pherber says.

"What do you mean?" Chas protests. "There's nothing wrong with me. I'm normal."

Pherber laughs and then taunts Chas, "How do you think Turner feels like?"

"I don't know; he's weird. And you're weird. You're kinky."

"He's a man. Male and female man." Pherber then tries to instill some "female feel" and "life gods" to Chas, but he is still sufficiently repressed to reject her efforts.

"I'm not one of those . . . . I said no . . . . you're sick . . . . you, you degenerate . . . . you're perverted." Chas screams. Then, shifting his focus to Turner, he asks, "What does he want to get out of my face? What does he want?"

"Maybe a mirror. A little dark mirror," Pherber answers.

"My mirror? No . . . . he shan't. He shan't. That's eating flesh." As Chas instinctively realizes that Turner's needs deeply involve him, Roeg cuts to a shot of Turner, hunched over the keyboards and apparently very aware of Chas and Pherber's conversation.

"He won't take it away, you fool," Pherber explains. "He just wants to take a look at it. He's stuck, stuck . . . . Because he's lost his demon. Yeh, he thought he had it under control, juggling all those balls, millions of them. Till one day, he was looking at his favorite mirror, admiring his image, see, and when suddenly he saw a bit too clearly that he was just a beautiful little freaky stripey beast, darling, so he thought maybe it's time for a change, he thought, and then immediately as he watched, the image faded. His demon had abandondoned him. He was gone. He's still trying to figure out whether he wants it back. He's gotta find it again."

"Listen," Chas interrupts, "I've got to tell you something."

"Go and tell him something. He's waiting for you. He's been waiting a long, long time. You must be polite."

Pherber and Chas's interaction in this scene is one of the most important and most lucid in the entire film. For one thing, it explains the film's preoccupation with mirrors and other reflecting devices. Mirrors figure in every scene. In the beginning of the movie, we think it is just a testament to Chas's narcissism. He looks at the mirror in his home, for example, to see how he would look with make-up. And when Harry takes his painting down to reveal a mirror, Chas reaches for his comb and makes sure that his hair is in place. But later, as Pherber plays with the mirror in bed and when Turner smashes the mirror to end the hallucination scene, and as Pherber explains their function, we see that mirrors are not just reflectors of how we look, but are the means by which we may affirm our existences. And, as a result, our images become not just illusions, but the roles that define these existences. As such, they are essential tools in the establishment of identities and identity transformations.

Pherber and Chas's interaction also shows how much Chas has changed. Although he still talks as if he is secure in knowing who he is, although he still asserts that he is clearly defined as a "man, a man all the time," he has become a willing participant in the relationship between Turner and himself. And when Pherber tells him to go to Turner, he does not protest. Instead, he gets up and willingly confronts Turner. He has come too far to do anything else.

When he meets with Turner, Chas finally confronts his repressed values and his long-suppressed female self. In this scene, he acknowledges his bisexuality and provides the opportunity for Turner and his physical, or sexual, merger, a merger that will prepare the way for their ultimate, psychic one.

We are not surprised by Chas's feelings for Turner, having been made aware of Chas's sexuality by the steady stream of homosexual references throughout the movie. When Chas looks in the mirror and imagines his lover's red beauty mark, he suggests a fascination with the more feminine side of himself. He works for Harry, a "pervert" with an extensive collection of homosexually oriented male magazines. The stag film Chas bursts in on depicts an act of anal intercourse, a position commonly associated with homosexuality. Chas calls himself a bullet, a label open to phallic and homoerotic implications. And Chas and Joey's relationship is referred to as being "double personal," which hints at a homosexual attraction. When Joey returns to Chas's apartment, he tries to make Chas admit that he is a "poof," a derogatory term for homosexuals. Also, Joey forces Chas to lie on his stomach and be whipped the same way the woman in the stag film was. To compound the erotic overtones of the action, Joey's whipping causes Chas to fantasize back to the film's initial love-making scene, an episode that left Chas's back scratched and bloodied in much the same way. Joey's helper picks up on the sexual tension between Chas and Joey, prompting him to call Joey's kissing of Chas the "kiss of life," another homosexual slang term.

Chas's hallucination confirms this uncomfortable attraction to-wards homosexuality. The hallucination is sparked by a psychedelic mushroom, which lowers Chas's defenses and ability to repress him-self, and by an erotic dance Turner performs for Chas. Since Chas is in drag and apparently at ease with his make-up, wig, and loose clothing and since Turner approaches him with a long, glowing fluorescent tube, the sexual imagery and implications become ines-capable. For the first time, Chas smiles at Turner, closes his eyes, and listens to Turner sing about a "faggy little leather boy," another reference to sado-masochistic homosexuality. Entranced by the song, Chas imagines a black and white picture of himself and Joey, embraced in a boyish street fight; the song's sensuality and Chas's reminiscence confirm our suspicions of a physical relationship be-tween Joey and Chas and also explain the intensity of their grudge.

The remainder of the hallucination is equally homoerotic. Chas watches all of the other gangsters take off their clothes, dance naked to Turner's song, and have sex with each other for "good old En-gland." We understand now that Chas is hardly as ignorant of this side of his sexuality as he seemed to be; even so, by the end of the hallucination, his body lies crumpled on the floor, exhausted and spent by its intensity.

The episode does not, however, end there. Roeg cuts to a shot of Pherber and Lucy in bed together, then to a shot of Chas and Turner in bed together. As they awaken, Turner rolls on top of Chas. As they embrace and kiss, Chas begins to pull off Turner's nightshirt. As he does, the body becomes Lucy's, the boyish French girl who lives with them. Whether Turner assumes Lucy's identity and Lucy Turner's or whether Chas has merely fantasized Turner next to him cannot be determined (probably due to James Fox's refusal to shoot a scene in bed with Jagger).[4] Regardless of who really is in bed with Chas, however, the scene shows Chas's deepening attraction to Turner and represents the final step in Chas's unification of his male and female selves.

Once this unification is effected, the final identity transfer can be made. When Chas goes up to Turner to tell him that "I've got to go now," Turner asks him to stay, saying that he "wants to talk to [Chas] some more." When Chas repeats that he has to go, Turner offers to go with him.

"You don't know where I'm going, pal," Chas says. "I do, I do," Turner slowly answers. The soundtrack's abstract music, propelled by the rhythm of a heartbeat, builds; Chas stares at Turner. As if suddenly scared, Turner changes his mind, "I don't know."

Chas continues to stare at Turner. Then, as if fully understanding for the first time, Chas says, "Yes, you do." And, recalling his earlier speech in which he describes himself as a "bullet," Chas raises a gun and shoots Turner in the head. But by killing Turner, or at least Turner's image, Chas has destroyed at least his own image and possibly himself. After all, in the film's final moments, we see Turner's lifeless body in a closet and also see Turner's face in the car window; we must assume that Turner has either taken over or merged with Chas's identity.

This identity transfer, which is primarily responsible for *Performance*'s difficulty and elusiveness, can be looked at in at least two ways. One way is to explain the ending as Chas's psychological projection of Turner, not unlike Norman Bates's experience in *Psycho*. The other way is to see it as an actual identity exchange, along the lines of those exchanges practiced by the pods in *The Invasion of the Body Snatchers*.

Using rational, naturalistic criteria, the psychological projection theory makes the most sense. Chas is an unstable anachronism, a narcissistic, old-fashioned, slightly paranoid, repressed, and violent gangster. Forced to flee for his survival and deprived of the emotional outlet that his work provided, he is then thrust into a dislocating environment and forced to deal with hidden, volatile elements of his personality. Baffled by but undeniably attracted to Turner, Chas kills Turner, not just because he is sexually threatening, but also because Turner betrayed him, either accidentally or deliberately, when he leaked Chas's whereabouts to the mob. That

Chas would then kill Turner seems consistent with his violent and unstable personality. But, as with Newton's inability to escape from the video images in *The Man Who Fell to Earth*, Chas cannot get Turner out of his mind; he may destroy Turner's body but cannot rid himself of Turner's power. Thus, he projects Turner's image onto his; at least in his own head, Chas becomes Turner.

This interpretation is tempting because it satisfies a demand for reality and rationality by reaffirming the rational order of the universe by reasonably explaining the film's events. In addition to leaving us with a reassuring security (since we know what has happened, we can get on with our lives, business as usual), it also explains the film's title.

"I'll tell you something," Turner says, "the only performance that makes it, that really makes it, that makes it all the way, is the one that achieves madness." Throughout the film, we have watched Chas confront hidden and obscure parts of himself in his efforts to adapt to the new norms of Turner's world. He takes drugs, even imagines that Lucy, his bed partner, is Turner. And when at the end he kills Turner and then projects Turner's image, his final performance, that of becoming Turner (even if only to himself), is certainly mad enough to "make it."

While comforting because so clear, however, this view of *Performance* is acceptable only by ignoring the atmosphere and specific images of the movie. Unlike Robert Altman's *Images*, for example, which becomes increasingly tangled and ambiguous with each viewing, repeated screenings of *Performance* reveal a logical, even linear narrative structure. We know, for instance, that Chas is a gangster who is outdated, see why Harry has to kill him, see how Chas gets to Turner's house, see how he gradually changes, and even see how he is exposed. We see him eat the mushroom and see him drift into and snap out of his hallucination. Thus, at least until that scene with Turner/Lucy in the bed and the final shot of Turner's face, *Performance* becomes a relatively straightforward movie.

There is also less thematic ambiguity than expected. From the first scene, Roeg carefully outlines the concept of identity transference. The presence of all the mirrors, the lawyer and Harry's talks of takeovers and mergers, the jury turning into the audience, the visual associations between Turner, Joey, and Chas, the conversations about what Chas would do if he were Turner, the merger of Chas and Pherber with the mirrors, the nature of homosexual love, where two similar bodies meet, even Turner's name (Turn er), all prepare us for the identity transfer.

More important than all these incidents are the speeches and events dealing with Turner's fascination with images. Although Turner and Pherber immediately see through Chas's facade of being an entertainer (when Chas explains his battered appearance to Pherber as a result of an automobile accident, Pherber sees through the lie and taunts him about his Ferrarri), they are intrigued by Chas's "image." When Chas comes down to the kitchen after washing the red dye out of his hair, Chas laughs. "Havin' a laugh, havin' a laugh with my act, with my image. Know what I mean?"

"Yeah, I know exactly what you mean," Turner answers convincingly.

"Thought you would," Chas answers. "He reckons, my agent, that is, that it's time for a change."

"Time for a change," Turner repeats. As he says this, his face becomes superimposed onto Chas's; their words mingle as well. Although the interchange is only momentary, it marks the beginning of the identity transfer. From this point on, Turner knows everything about Chas, including his real name, his profession, and his reason for hiding. And Chas begins to experiment with his image, wearing a hat, women's clothes, and make-up.

. Although he starts to delve into his inner psyche under their care, however, Chas remains suspicious of Turner and Pherber's motives. And when he finds out that they have drugged him, he screams that they have "poisoned" him.

"I just want to go in there, Chas," Turner reassures him. "You see, the blood of this vegetable [the mushroom] is boring a hole. This second hole is penetrating the hole [whole] of your face, the skull of your bones. I just want to get right in there, do you know what I mean, and root around in there."

Although Chas should be remembering his own advice to the lawyer, "to shut your hole," Pherber gives him little time to think, instantaneously picking up Turner's refrain. "C'mon, you're beautiful," she tells him. "We just want to dismantle you a little bit, that's all."

"Just to see how you function." Turner adds.

Pherber continues, only a little more malevolently, "we sat through your act. Now you're gonna sit through ours."

Despite Turner and Pherber's protestations that they mean no harm, Turner's actions belie their words. In a ritualistic motion, he takes two knives that are pointing towards each other in, perhaps, a symbolic representation of merger, and turns one around. Both knives are now pointing in the same direction; rather than a mutually beneficial exchange, they now become a suggestion of take-over. And since we have seen through Harry's actions what merger and take-over really mean, we realize that Chas's fears and distrust of Turner are justified.

As the film progresses, Chas and Turner become even more intertwined. Pherber, Lucy, Turner, and, eventually, Chas all go to bed with each other. By the end, then, the four are sufficiently involved both psychically and physically to make Chas sense that Turner knows everything about the gangsters and the execution (thus explaining why Chas does not believe Turner when Turner claims he does not know where Chas is going). When Chas shoots Turner, he does so by putting a hole into Turner's head, just as Chas put one into Joey's head and as Turner put one into Chas's. As the bullet goes further and further into Turner's core, it reaches a mirror that has in it a picture of an old man (in reality, Borges, the film's patron saint). Presumably he is Turner's demon, now recaptured. But the bullet does not stop there; it passes through and goes outside and beyond the mirror. And as the bullet goes through the mirror, it magically redefines reality and affects the identity transfer.

Thus, Chas becomes what he repeatedly claimed to be, a bullet and, as a bullet, the agent of Turner's renewal. Through a very lengthy and deliberate process, Turner has merged identities, or at least images, with Chas. While Turner's old body lies discarded in the closet, perhaps with Chas's spirit, Turner and his new image are free to leave. And although Chas did get to unify his male and female selves and acquired a taste for the bohemian atmosphere, he in the end becomes just one more example of someone suffering a merger that is really a take-over.

When Turner assumes Chas's identity, he acts no differently from Harry in the beginning of the movie. But the link between Harry and Turner proves to be more than one of similar methods. Indeed, when the relationship between Harry and Turner is explored, the true impact of the film is unleashed.

Although Harry and Turner are linked together in many ways

TOP: Chas at work—and play.

BOTTOM: The triangle.

throughout the movie, the most obvious linkage is Turner's insistence that Chas call his "agent," Tony. After forcing Chas—who is still feeling the effects of the drug and the hallucination—to make the phone call, Turner, not Chas, reveals the address to Tony. This information lets the gang find Chas and eventually leads to Turner's own liberation from the image he has been stuck in.

Even more suspect than the fact that Turner benefits from the gangsters' appearance is the fact that he knows Chas is not a juggler, but is a fugitive from the mob. He figures out that Chas needs the photo for his passport, knows what Chas did, and, in his reading of a Borges short story, predicts the arrival of the executioners. Yet, although he knows all this, he still insists that Chas call Tony and then himself divulges the address, not just once, but three times. That Turner is connected with the gangsters in some way, then, seems inescapable.

Also, when Chas is being taken into the car, Rosie, another of Flower's gangsters, goes to the basement and leaves a note for Lucy. "Gone to Persia. X Chas." We never see Chas write the note; while it is possible that he wrote it, it is just as likely that Turner, who was more familiar with Lucy's dreams of Persia, wrote it. After all, Chas has just killed Turner and is himself being dragged off to die; that he would remember a passing suggestion from Lucy is debatable. If, however, Rosie is connected to Turner and since Turner is not caught up in a traumatic but a celebratory experience, Turner, now in Chas's image, would be more likely to write that note.

The connection between Flowers and Turner is more conclusively suggested by their tendency to have identical observations and expressions. Harry calls Chas an "artist," a description that Turner also uses. More convincing is repeated use of the phrase, "He's got the gift. He enjoys his work." We first hear it used by Harry and Denny as they reprimand Chas for interfering with Joey Maddox. Pherber is the next to say it, telling Chas that "you enjoy your work, heh. You've got the gift." Turner also repeats it, using "They enjoyed their work" as the last phrase of the story about the assassins, a story that applies to Chas as much as to the gangsters who come to take him away.

Another verbal interchange that is repeated by both is the one about the buttons. "I'm alive and well," Chas tells Harry, "you push the buttons on that." "Right, we push them." Harry answers. Later, Chas tells Turner, "I'm alive and well. You push the buttons." And just as Harry has, Turner understands and responds, "We push the buttons."

This verbal connection, which at the very least points to a metaphoric similarity between Harry and Turner's roles, is enhanced by a strange visual image in the film. We see Chas talking on the phone to Harry, see Harry cover the phone and hear him pronounce Chas's death sentence, and see Chas draw a picture of himself as a hanged man. Soon afterwards, as Chas is waiting for a train that will take him out of London, he overhears a black musician talking to his white mother about his now vacant room at Turner's. Although the coincidence of the conversation, especially the way in which the address is dropped into it, is in itself curious, Chas quickly gets up and heads for Turner's. Then, as Chas approaches the house, Roeg cuts to a disturbed Harry, who is looking directly into the camera. The inescapable implication is that Harry knows who Turner is and that Chas is heading there, as if according to plan.

These ties would remain tenuous or even just coincidental were it not for the hallucination scene. For in it, the connection between Flowers and Turner is made explicit; Turner sits at Harry's desk and controls Harry's men. He has a sexual power and leadership over the group that Harry can never have; when Turner sneers at the men at the end of the hallucination and says, "Remember, you all work for me," we believe it. And since Harry by this time has walked into the office and since he remains powerless against Turner's proclamation, we can only assume that Harry, too, works for Turner.

Because this is happening in Chas's hallucination, Harry and Turner's relationship could be argued as being a strictly metaphoric one, representing only a reworking in Chas's mind of the conference Harry has with Chas earlier in the film and of the similar power Turner now has over him. As such, then, all the hallucination proves is Chas's mental connection between Harry and Turner. There is, however, a curious detail in the hallucination scene that proves an actual and not just metaphoric relationship between the two men.

When Harry sits in his office, he sits in front of a painting of a horseback rider (who looks a lot like Harry) who is dressed in a red riding outfit. There is, however, another painting in the film. Shortly after Chas arrives at Turner's, two men in tunics bring him a painting of a disembodied head (that looks like Fraser, Harry's ex-partner who is now on trial) in front of some classical architecture.

Turner tells them he cannot afford to buy it; the two men leave with the painting. Chas, who does not want to be seen by anyone, hides from the two men the entire time they are in Turner's house; he has no way of seeing the painting.

In the hallucination scene, however, Turner sits in Harry's chair; behind him is not the painting of the horseback rider, which we would expect Chas to associate with Harry's office, but the painting of the man's head. If this were not strange enough, when Harry enters the hallucination scene, he brings the red rider painting with him. We see Turner go into a private room to have sex with one of the men; when Roeg pans back to the office, the red rider painting is back in its place, replacing the new painting. But when Turner reminds them that they all work for him, he casually tosses the red painting away and smashes the mirror behind it.

The juxtaposition of the paintings indicates some sort of power hierarchy; that Turner replaces Harry's painting and then, when it is put back, discards it, reaffirms the accuracy of Turner's announcement; they do work for him. And since Chas has never seen the painting, he cannot be expected to project it into his fantasy. Its presence here, then, does help objectify the hallucination and add credibility to the existence of an actual relationship between Turner and the gangsters.

Finally, when Turner finishes his song, just before he reminds them that they work for him, he sings that "the baby's dead." In the context of the song it means nothing—until we remember Harry's motto, "After death, who's left holding the sodden baby?" (Harry, of course.) At the time, Harry's announcement made as little sense as Turner's lyric; when treated together, however, the meaning becomes much clearer. After all the excitement and action, Harry must tie up the loose ends, take care of the aftermath. And, just before reminding Harry that he is still the boss, Turner tells him that the baby is dead and that it is time for Harry to get busy.

The relationship between Harry and Turner is important because it links the first half of the film to the second half, proving little difference between the business world and the personal one. There are, however, even more interesting and more unambiguous incidents in *Performance* that point to Turner's almost demonic control over the film's events and over Chas's fate.

There is, of course, all the talk of images, of how Turner wants to give Chas a "new image," something "totally different" from his old one. And we know from Pherber that Turner needs a new image; from Harry that if the change involves a merger, it also means a takeover. We also know that Turner's world is dark and threatening and that Chas consider himself a bullet, or an agent of execution. Furthermore, Turner sings a song about Chas's entry into Turner's world: "Woke up this morning. Someone knocking on my door. Hello, Satan—I believe it's time to go." In other words, from the beginning, Turner planned to use Chas as his escape from his own stuck image. That this is in his mind becomes chillingly unavoidable with the song's next line, "I'm going to shoot you"; Chas may pull the trigger but he will be the one who is ultimately destroyed.

Because Chas is going to provide Turner with his new image, Turner draws Chas out, carefully getting Chas to talk about and explain how he really feels about himself and his image. It is not, however, an easy task; Turner must first bait Chas. "He knows who he is," Turner begins. "He's the horror show. He's an old pro. He can take it. He takes it, dishes it out too—you bet your sweet fucking life he does. He's a mean bastard." Later, Turner will tell Chas that he (Turner) has "been on the road a million years . . . . a million years people have been comin' in and draggin' in to watch. I know how you do it. I know a thing or two about performing, boy."

When Chas complains, Pherber explains that Turner has been milking Chas only because "he wants to know why your show's a bigger turn on than his ever was." To which Chas answers, in one of his most honest speeches in the movie, "How should I know? I know a thing or two about the clientele; they're a bunch of liars and wrigglers—put the frighteners on them—give them a bit a' stick— that's the way to make them jump. They love it."

Turner now has what he wants; he greets the admission with "Time for your new image. Totally different." To which Pherber adds, "Now we're getting somewhere." Thus, Turner, who sees himself as an old man whose act has grown stale, discovers everything about Chas's image, or act. And under a disguise of a disinterested observer, he proceeds to merge with, steal, or take over that image.

The malevolence of Turner's intentions is amplified by the film's references to Satan and to Turner being one million or one thousand years old and by his pretense of merely wanting to look inside Chas's head. These individual incidents are finally pulled together when Turner reads from Argentinian short story writer Jorge Luis Borges'

"The Old Man on the Mountain." In the story, an old man establishes a paradise to which he lures young assassins. These assassins are given a potion and then supplied with "damsels and gardens," everything young men want. They then are trained to go out and kill princes; when they are done, the angels (or damsels) return them to paradise. And the young men? They "enjoyed their work."

The parallels are obvious. Turner, whom Chas at the beginning of their relationship describes as a "comical little geezer," is the old man; the house is paradise; Lucy and Pherber, the damsels; the mushrooms, the potion the old man gives the assassins. As we shall see, Turner is also the prince. And, of course, Chas, who has been told that he enjoys his work so many times, is one of the young men.

If the implication were not clear enough, Pherber asks Chas if he is "in the garden." When he tells her he is, she begs him to "Stay there. Never trust old men, old show men, old wankers." Then, as if she has admitted too much and has no real voice anyway, she sighs. "I might take you down to the riverside [Turner will also tell Chas that], I might powder you, I might polish you, I might make you shiny like a mirror. I just don't know."

Since what Turner wants of Chas is a mirror, "a dark mirror," Pherber's function and her warning are unmistakable. She is preparing Chas for the identity transfer, a process that was begun the moment Chas heard about Turner's, if not before. Which explains all the demonic imagery and threatening atmospheres and discussions; Turner is after Chas's image and has been since their first meeting.

Ultimately, this vaguely threatening and evil atmosphere is what makes *Performance* so powerful and compelling. It is a film that carefully sets its stage, obscuring hints and relationships, suggesting motivations, establishing connections by innuendo. Its world is one of imagination, not naturalism; of Persia, not London or New York; of art, not science or economics. It introduces Chas and us in the audience to theater, roles, acts, images, and illusions, to painting, music, dance, and drugs. And all are used so that Chas's emotions can be liberated and unified; even if he must in some way die from the exposure, he at least performs, experiences, creates, And although he must die, the alternative, being stuck, living like Turner as a prisoner of his own and old image, does not seem that much more different or attractive.

Which at last brings us back to the title of the film, *Performance*.

As we have seen, this film is not a conventional one; it does not have the epic sweep of a movie like *Lawrence of Arabia* or even of *Star Wars*. Moreover, none of the characters is especially engaging; we have no one really to root for or pin our own fates to. So then, who or what are we supposed to be identifying with, to whom are we supposed to be relating?

A look at the film's style provides the answer. For in addition to making the plot all but undecipherable, at least for the first one or two viewings, Roeg uses extremely obtrusive cinematography and editing; he has characters looking and talking directly to us in the audience; he has us almost constantly asking, "did you see that?" These are not the devices of a director who wants to remain invisible or foster the illusion that what is on the screen is "real life." No, instead they indicate a director who wants us to watch, identify with, and finally participate in his own performance, his own creative act. Because his performance as director involves all aspects of film, not just acting or cinematography or the screenplay, he hides none of the elements. In fact, he flamboyantly incorporates them into the design of the film. And although this is a very dangerous strategy, Roeg has enough talent, taste, and artistic integrity to make it become a challenging but very effective series of visual images.

Especially in the first part of the film, before Chas arrives at Turner's, for instance, Roeg makes almost exorbitant visual demands on the viewer, presenting a number of events and characters with no verbal or outside explanation and with little apparent reason for the intercutting. But as soon as we adjust to the film's rapid pace and learn to recognize the individual characters, we do not need the narration and begin to feel the connections between Harry, the lawyer, Chas, Joey, and the other gangsters. Rather than begin as most would with a meeting and then with flashbacks or dialogue to explain the relationships and events, Roeg begins as they each prepare for their meetings. Thus, by the time the characters actually meet, we have seen each of their personalities and can grasp their interrelationships. Simply by placing the lawyer's car next to Chas's violent love-making, for example, Roeg subconsciously and visually prepares us for Chas's violent personality, for the interrelationship of sex with power, and for the actual extent of Chas's revenge against the lawyer. And it is all done through the use of creative editing of selected visuals, not by the more theatrical, literary, and verbal conventions of dialogue, character, and plot development.

This does not mean that words play no part in the film, just that at least in the first part of the film they are used to support the visuals. When establishing the relationship between the lawyer, Harry, and Chas, Roeg uses the lawyer's semantic discussion of mergers and takeovers to provide the continuity as he cuts from one character to the next. As we watch Chas smash machines and beat up people and see Harry plan to absorb Joey Maddox's operation, we hear the lawyer's words—until they too are drowned out by the noises of unseen computers. Roeg thus makes his comments through his editing; because of his placement of the visuals and soundtrack, we know that the three of them are involved in takeovers or, as they would prefer to call them, mergers.

Roeg uses the camera the same creative way he edits. Rather than take time to describe directly Chas's relationship to Harry and Harry's to Denny, his legal advisor, for example, Roeg shoots Chas in a noticeably high angle and shoots Harry in a wide angle, telling us immediately that Harry has gross but overwhelming and inescapable power over Chas. And to convey Harry's relative powerlessness and Denny's influence over Harry, Roeg cuts to a shot of Harry's moving lips. While that is all we see of Harry, Denny remains in the background in full view and sharp focus. Harry, despite his position, is no more than a puppet himself. In two simple shots, then, Roeg establishes the power hierarchy of the mob and is free to go on to other things. Another example of Roeg's creative camera and visuals occurs when Harry talks about how he is left holding the "baby" after the henchmen die. A morally bankrupt argument, his words are accompanied by the loss of Harry and Denny's flesh color; by the time Harry is finished speaking, a green tint gives the two men a corpse-like appearance that effectively and immediately communicates their moral decadence and emptiness.

Unfortunately, though, and as this analysis, which has been forced to draw so extensively from the dialogue, shows, Roeg's efforts to keep *Performance* visual are not entirely successful. As a visual experience, the film is so dense and so demanding that the viewer is overwhelmed; rather than being able to interact emotionally with much of the film, we spend too much time trying to figure out what is happening. And too often that confusion is alleviated only by paying careful attention to key speeches. Without the explanation of the loss of Turner's image, without the talk of mergers and takeovers, and without the Borges excerpts, the second half of *Performance* would be almost totally incomprehensible. Roeg will learn how to tell an atmospheric story more strictly visually by the time he makes *Don't Look Now;* in his first directorial effort, however, Roeg's ability to keep his film visual rather than verbal is still developing.

Perhaps because the dialogue becomes so crucial to the second part of the movie, Roeg cannot sustain the pace of the film's first sequences. By the time Chas gets to Turner's, we are accustomed to the rapid rhythm of the film. When Roeg shifts his focus from Chas, the bullet, to Turner, the film slows down. Not only does the set become confined to Turner's dark, grotesque house, but the action, reduced to the confrontation between Chas and Turner, takes on a more static, more verbal, and more mystical tone. Although reflective of Turner's personality and dominant position in this part of the film and therefore structurally justified, the strangeness and oppressiveness of the second part too often overwhelm us. And when that happens, Roeg tends to lose us.

Performance's excessiveness, self-indulgence, and precociousness is, however, most forgiveable because it stems from the most artistic and ambitious of sensibilities. Even if the film is uneven, even if it never is integrated into a fully coherent whole, there are enough brilliant sequences in *Performance* to make it a very powerful and original viewing experience. So, even though Roeg will later learn to let his visuals convey his ideas and emotions more thoroughly and will not shift his rhythm so radically in the middle of the film (with the possible exception of *The Man Who Fell* to Earth's incarceration scene), *Performance* still has enough vitality and identity to remain a triumph in its own right. In fact, its visual style, complexity, and boldness just might make it the most exciting directoral debut since Orson Welles's *Citizen Kane*.

3

Walkabout

SO THE BOY SAID, "I have to be getting home from work." He lived with his mother on the house on top of the hill. She had never spoken to him; he'd never heard her say a word. He thought she was dumb and she was blind, too, but this evening, when he came up the hill, he saw her sitting at the window and she was talking but once he put his key in the lock, she would stop. And when he got inside, she wouldn't say a word.

So, one evening, he made up his mind to hear what she was saying. So he put the ladder . . . . oh, yes, he went around the back and got the ladder and he . . . . carried it around to the front of the house and set it up against the window . . . . It was very, very long and heavy and he only just managed to get it in position in front of the house. Next, he climbed up the ladder and he got on the windowsill, but he couldn't hear a word. She was only a few feet away behind the window and her blind eyes were staring straight at him and her mouth was opening and shutting but he couldn't hear because she was speaking silently to herself. So he put his ear to the glass but he still couldn't hear it so he decided to come down. But the windowsill was very narrow and when he came around, he knocked the ladder down. So he was stuck—he couldn't jump down because it was too far and he couldn't shout to his mother because then she would know he'd been spying on her . . . .

It got dark and because there wasn't much room on the sill, his legs grew very stiff. Sometimes people went past but he couldn't shout for help because his mother would hear. So there was a drainpipe going down the wall and the boy thought if I reach across and get hold of that, I'll be able to climb down. So he reached across—but he slipped off the windowsill and fell down and broke his neck!   (from *Walkabout*)

At first glance, *Walkabout*, Roeg's second film, looks so simple that it seems like an apology for *Performance's* complexity, intellectualism, and avant-garde sexuality. When *Walkabout* is examined, however, it reveals itself to be much more than a simple little nature story about two children lost in the Australian desert and the aborigine youth who leads them to safety. Instead, it becomes an intricately structured and objective commentary on the effects civilization has on its members. And while the message and narrative here may be much more accessible than in *Performance*, Roeg's presentation is still surprisingly sophisticated.

The film begins with a disjointed and very fast montage of modern urban life. Geometric and sterilely beautiful patterns of concrete give way to shots of traffic jams, crowds of people, ground kangaroo meat in antiseptic plastic wrapping, and rows of schoolgirls bouncing up and down in their school-desks and panting in unison. Next, a boy, on his way home from school, leaves the sidewalk and enters a lush park. As the boy goes into the park, Roeg switches to a wide angle lens, which gives the greenery an unnatural, distorted, almost artificial appearance. And although the trees are healthy and beautiful, we notice that each wears a botanical name tag. It is as if they are no longer part of the natural order, but are artifacts in a living museum, reminders of a world no longer alive. After seeing the degree to which man has imposed his order on nature, we are not surprised that although the boy's apartment complex stands directly on the ocean, he and his sister swim in a man-made pool built right next to the water.

The city people are divorced not just from nature, but from each other as well. We never see them socializing, laughing, or playing, for example, but only as anonymous components of unsmiling crowds. When the boy's father (none of the characters in the film will be given names) returns home from work, he does not greet, kiss, or even talk to his wife; he just stares at her. When he speaks to his children, it is to reprimand them, to tell them not to "chew with [their] mouths open" or to turn the radio down. And even then, his commands are conveyed more through hostile glares and threatening gestures than through his words.

However cold, structured, and drab city life seems to be, though, it still seems more inviting than the wilderness, the barren desert that lies beyond the red brick wall separating the civilized world from the primitive one. Even with all the concrete and crowds, the city looks less threatening than our first glimpses of the endless, brown desert filled only with sand, lizards, and snakes.

The children in *Walkabout* do not, of course, enter the desert for fun, by choice, or with preparation. As the radio in the film will later say, it was not a "question of free will," but of "that that is, is." Their father drives them out into the desert, tries for some unexplained reason to kill them, and, after he fails, kills himself. And so that she and her younger brother do not have to walk past the burning car and their father's bloody body, the girl leads them away from the car and deeper into the wilderness.

From the beginning of their confrontation with the natural world of the desert, the boy and the girl react differently. The boy, younger and less socialized, acts childishly and poorly at first. Lacking discipline and an awareness of the dangers inherent in their situation, he quickly becomes irritable, self-centered, and discouraged. When he rolls down a sand dune, for instance, he refuses to get up. Pretending to be too weak to get up, he tricks his equally exhausted sister into carrying him. The older, more mature girl, however, makes a noble, even heroic effort at returning to civilization. Extremely sensitive to her brother's less persevering mental and physical capabilities, she thinks up games to keep him moving and tries to remain cheerful and optimistic. In response to the seriousness of their plight, she taps an admirable resourcefulness, opening a can of cherries with a rock, seeking high ground to search for lights, and remembering an old uncle's story about how he licked salt when he was lost in the desert.

No matter how clever, selfless, and courageous she is, however, she is no match for the desert. The environment is totally alien to her and her brother; they have no way of knowing, for example, that the oasis will dry up overnight or that the birds will eat all the fruit while the children sleep. Regardless of her mental attitude, then, she is not equipped to cope with the desert; without minimal information, she could not be expected to survive.

Although she brings no information to the walkabout, she does bring to her ordeal an entire set of attitudes and habits that prohibit her from being totally flexible and adaptable to the wilds. Unlike her younger, less socialized brother, the girl is very much a product of an advanced Anglican civilization; her insistence on keeping a stiff upper lip and an immaculate, respectable appearance may give her a will to move forwards and not to give up, but it also leads to an unnatural and inappropriate sense of modesty and formality. Thus, she takes great care with their clothes, washing and pressing them at every opportunity. (At the end of the film, they look brand new.) When, after two grueling days, the children stumble onto the oasis, the boy happily takes his clothes off and jumps into the pond. The girl, on the other hand, has already internalized society's codes of propriety; in keeping with these standards, she keeps her slip and bra on, contenting herself with a less refreshing and, under the circumstances, somewhat absurd sponge bath. Her reluctance to undress in front of her brother is the first clear indication of her sexual repression, a repression that will ultimately create insurmountable barriers between herself and the aborigine and that will prevent her from fully enjoying her experience.

The extent of her socialization becomes apparent during her first meeting with the aborigine. She has given up and is waiting to die when, to the swirl of some obtrusive and decidedly religious soundtrack music, the aborigine emerges from the horizon. Realizing that he will know where to get some water, the boy and girl run up to him. She asks the aborigine to get her some water but since he has no reason to speak English, he does not understand her. His failure to understand frustrates the girl; instead of trying to show him what she means, she just repeats "water" in increasingly louder and demanding tones. She finally becomes hysterical. "Water, we need water. Surely you can understand that, anyone can understand that!" As the aborigine, who still does not know what she is talking and screaming about, turns to leave, the boy points to his mouth and makes drinking noises. "Guapa, guapa," laughs the aborigine, bending down to show them how to draw water from the ground.

Even though the girl should know how to communicate more effectively than the boy, then, her insistence on the aborigine understanding her language and attuning himself automatically to her frame of reference demonstrates a deep seated imperialistic prejudice engrained in the girl. The boy, who has been less indoctrinated, is, on the other hand, much more open and willing to communicate with the aborigine on the aborigine's own terms. Thus, he instantly learns where the water is; in the following days, he will delightedly imitate the aborigine's movements and dress, will learn the aborigine's language, and will adapt to the aborigine's environment. By the end of the film, he will become an interpreter as well, translating his sister's words to the aborigine and the aborigine's to his sister.

The real reason for the distance between the aborigine and the girl is not national or even racial prejudice, but is a sexual tension between the two adolescents. The girl's self-consciousness is hinted at by her refusal to take her clothes off and bathe at the oasis; Roeg

An uncharacteristically happy moment.

makes her sexual fears explicit in the scene where the three play in
the trees. The aborigine hoists the boy into a group of trees. As the
boy swings through the branches, his laughter sweeps the girl into
the game. As the aborigine lifts her up to the branch, however, the
girl makes a self-conscious effort at keeping her legs crossed so that
the aborigine will not be able to see her underwear. As soon as she
gets up in the tree, though, she relaxes and is able to have fun.
Unfortunately, it is one of the few times in the film that we shall see
her so happy.

In the film's next moments, Roeg tells us why. After they get
down from the trees, the girl looks at the tree trunks. Under her
gaze, the music becomes softer and more romantic and the branches
of the trees become almost human, erotic images of arms, legs, and
crotches. Especially when tied to her earlier, furtive glances at the
aborigine's waist and her embarrassed refusal to finish her statement
that [her body] "got a bit sore from—oh, dear," playing on the tree,
the girl's behavior has unmistakable sexual implications. But rather
than face her sexuality directly, the girl hides from it, replacing the
innocence and fun of the tree game with guilt and a false reserve.

So that she does not have to confront the sexual problem, she
avoids any prolonged contact with the aborigine. While the "men"
hunt, pitch camp, clean the meat, and cook, she lounges alone by
the campsite; only then does she relax, take off her clothes, go
swimming. When she does interact, she usually keeps her manner
within a maternal role, warning her brother not to take his shirt off
or, later, reminding him that had he listened, he would not now be
so sunburned. Although she tells her brother not to bother telling
the aborigine a story that he cannot possibly understand, she does
not mind interrupting the boy's recitation of it, correcting his details, adding parts he left out, and pointing out inconsistencies in his
version.

In addition to making her irritable, the girl's fears lead to her
refusal to become involved with the aborigine's culture. Her
brother begs to be painted from head to toe with the aborigine's
body paint and responds immediately to the aborigine's art, which
depicts spaceships and men falling to earth. The girl, however,
whose advanced education should have prepared her for the amazing implications the pictures suggest, refuses to be moved. Instead,
she complains that they do not even have real crayons and paint and
closes herself off to any new feelings and experiences.

At times, her childish behavior assumes imperialistic and racist dimensions, as well. When they come across the abandoned house, the girl and the aborigine, who both realize that their walkabout is ending, look into each other's eyes. Finally, they make honest, tender, and moving contact with each other. But, once again fleeing from the sexual possibilities the moment may lead to, the girl destroys the mood by insensitively commanding him to get her some "guapa." Although her tone is haughty, the aborigine smiles; it is the first time the girl has spoken to him in his language. To return the gesture, he responds for the first time in English; "water," he proudly says. But rather than acknowledging this use of his English, rather than thanking him for saving her and her brother and taking them back to civilization, she coldly turns away, dismissing him as if he were an ignorant, inconsequential, and unskilled servant and she an elegant Victorian lady.

Shortly thereafter, when he begins his strange dance and sees her without her blouse on, she becomes terrified, fearing that he will rape her or at the very least force her to respond to her own sexual feelings. Rather than act with trust, intelligence, or maturity, she madly slams doors in the aborigine's face and huddles in the corner. She almost screams when the door finally opens; to her relief, it is her brother and not the aborigine who comes in.

As frightened as she is, however, she retains enough control, propriety, and maternal protectiveness to still be able to protect her brother from what she fears. When the boy repeatedly demands to know what the aborigine's dance means, she replies euphemistically and, as it turns out, ironically, "maybe it's his way of saying good-bye." So that she will not have to explain any further, she tries to turn her brother against the aborigine and begins preparing her brother for their return to civilization. The aborigine has served his purpose and now must be disposed of.

The girl's reaction to the aborigine's death tells us more about her relationship to him. When the brother discovers the aborigine's body and tells her about it, the girl treats the death very matter-of-factly. "Did you eat your breakfast properly?" she asks her brother as they stare at the corpse. "You should always sit down when you eat and not wander about." Once again, though, she may be simply trying to protect her brother; we can see by her eyes and facial expression that she cares about the aborigine a great deal. And before she leaves him, she gently touches his chest and flicks the flies off it; despite the cultural differences and her sexual fears and her distance, the aborigine has touched her deeply.

Regret over the aborigine is mitigated, however, by her eagerness to get back to civilization, "to have a warm bath with clean towels, to eat with real knives, plates and forks, to have proper sheets and records." She quickly finds out, though, that civilization is more than fancy silverware and soft sheets. For when they arrive at the almost deserted town, the lone inhabitant is indifferent to their ordeal and needs and is somewhat unbelievably concerned only that they do not disturb his or the company's property. However comfortable and reassuring the idea of civilization may have seemed to her in the desert, its reality is as harsh as the desert's.

We quickly find out how harsh; from a shot of the two children in a junk yard trying to flag down a ride, Roeg swish pans and flash forwards to the city, several years later. The girl is now married and preparing dinner in the same city, apartment, and kitchen that her mother occupied in the beginning of the movie. Perhaps because they are still young, the girl's husband does not ignore her. Instead, as he comes home from work, hugs her and tells her about a reshuffling in his office that will mean a raise and a promotion, she ignores him. As he rambles on, the girl remembers her walkabout. She visualizes her brother and herself naked on a mud bank in the middle of a pond. In her reminiscence, the aborigine smiles, dives into the water, and swims towards them. Then, as the three laugh and play in harmony with nature and themselves, we hear a voice-over: "Into my heart an air that kills, from yon far country blows. What are those blue remembered hills, what spires, what farms are those? That is the land of lost content; I see it shining, playing the happy highways where I went and cannot come again." In her memory, the sexual fears have been replaced by a more natural, healthy attitude. If only that were the way it could have been—and could be now.

That her experience in the desert was a chance at a simpler, happier life-style is confirmed not just by the poem, but by the film's framing device. Before the film's first visual, a voice whispers in French, "faites vous jeux," the croupier's announcement that bets may be placed on the game. And at the very end of the movie, after the poem, after the credits, and after the final visual, the whisper returns; "re ne va plus," he tells us, the last chance to place the bets has passed. Positions have been taken; all that remains is to play them out to the end.

The message seems clear; the girl has refused her alternative to the city and has failed to take advantage of her chance for a more natural, more elemental life-style. And now she is trapped by the very civilization that she chose to return to. So all she is left with is her romanticized memory of "the happy highway" on which she went "and cannot come" upon again.

We cannot, however, blame the girl for returning from the desert; the notion of remaining in the wilderness may be compelling, but at no time is it a very realistic alternative. The girl is a child of modern society and as such belongs there, just as the aborigine belongs in the desert. As the film tells us, it is not a "question of free will," but of "that that is, is." She does not even have the freedom to react naturally anymore; even her repression can be traced to civilization's unhealthy influence.

As if to exonerate the girl from any sense of failure, Roeg deliberately moves the film outside the story of the three youths and makes more sweeping and comprehensive comparisons between urban civilization and the more primitive yet more natural aborigine society. The radio the children salvage from the car, for example, serves as a constant reminder of civilization's priorities, offering programs like "Hospital Requests," advice on what to do when a fish fork is not provided, prayers for Armistice Day, and strange comments like "after ten thousand years of trial and suffering . . . (do not expect that) there might at last be a perpetual succession of comfortable shopkeepers." Because of the radio in the background, then, we are rarely allowed to forget how petty civilization's concerns can be.

Roeg's use of the butcher continues his comment on civilization's true character. At the beginning of the film, a butcher prepares meat that has already been sanitized, sectioned, and ground. The final product bears little resemblance to the animal it once was; the butcher has become a specialist performing a small step in the complicated process that brings modern man his food. The aborigine, however, kills and cleans the kangaroo himself and uses every part of the animal, if not for food then for tools and materials for his daily life. As the aborigine separates meat and tendons from the bone, Roeg intercuts to another urban butcher who is making chops from a larger section of meat. Once again we are impressed with the fragmentation of modern civilization, especially when contrasted with the relative simplicity and self-sufficiency of the aborigine's life-style. At the end of the movie, we see the girl preparing some pre-cleaned, packaged meat; although she saw in the walkabout the total process, she too must now adhere to civilization's more fragmented processes.

The scene where the three children play in the trees does not just tell us of the girl's sexual feelings, but also tells us more about the aborigine's world and the white children's. In it, the girl tells her brother to give the aborigine one of his toy soldiers; "I expect he'd like to play," she says. "He's never had any toys of his own." Moments later, we see that the aborigine may not have wooden soldiers, fake guns, or model airplanes, but is able to have fun by playing with the natural environment, by using the trees as his toy.

While they play, Roeg cuts to a group of aborigines who have discovered one of civilization's toys, the girl's father's burnt-out car. Although they probably do not know what the car is, the aborigines seem to be enjoying crawling in and out of it. In both cases, however, the games are short-lived, prematurely concluded because of civilization's intrusions. The girl's sexual associations destroy the innocence and fun of playing in the trees, while the car radio, accidentally turned on by an aborigine, scares the aborigines away from the car with its disembodied voice.

Before the radio frightens them away, however, the aborigines discover the decomposing, half-eaten body of the father. Rather than let him lie on the ground, they hang his body in a tree, where it will be safe from ground animals. Especially when compared to the insanity of the father, the mistreatment of the children by the old man in the mining town, and the carnage of the hunters, the aborigines' simple respect for another living creature gives them a dignity and decency absent in members of the more advanced technological society.

The contrast between urban life and nature is made not just thematically, but also through the film's editing. The urban montages are disjointed, confusing, and unrelated except by the themes of anonymity and directionless, perpetual motion. Buildings, cars, and people move by at a rapid pace, giving us little time to sort out our sensory impressions. Once in the desert, however, Roeg uses a more fluid, more relaxed editing style. In this section of the movie, he allows dissolves, freeze frames, and slow motion, all of which lend a lyrical quality to the film and enhance the natural beauty of the environment. In the final scene, which combines Roeg's comment on the city with the girl's daydream of the desert, Roeg continues his characterizations through editing. The shots of the city are as jarring and as quick as the introductory montage; as soon as the girl remembers the aborigine, however, Roeg returns to an appropriately leisurely pace and to the almost unrestrained use of dissolves. Thus, because the pace of the city is so much more fragmented and hectic than the desert's, Roeg edits the city scenes much more quickly and nervously than the more tranquil and flowing nature scenes.

The film's most sophisticated and comprehensive condemnation of civilization revolves around the use of freeze frames in three different but related sequences. The first time a freeze frame is used is when the aborigine stalks and kills the kangaroo. As the aborigine spears the animal, Roeg freezes it, the aborigine, a bird, and the boy. When the kangaroo dies, Roeg shifts to a high grain film stock, as if to document the moment of death. But rather than make the death disgusting, it gives the moment a strange dignity because it is such a real fact of life. To prove that the aborigine is acting in harmony with nature, the animal's death does not disturb the other animals, nor are there shrieks of pain, terror, and panic. To emphasize the ecological necessity and beauty of the aborigine's actions, Roeg cuts back to the butcher in the city making chops. Unlike the aborigine, the butcher is divorced from the natural setting and from the whole picture; because he does not seem to be in tune with the balance of nature, he has none of the aborigine's aura of self-sufficiency and harmony with nature.

Roeg uses freeze frames again at the science station. All of a sudden, out of nowhere, comes a red balloon belonging, we find out, to a meterorological research team. Rather than be defined by their function or their personalities, however, the six men and one woman who make up the team are defined entirely by the men's adolescent, sexist reactions. Oblivious to their surroundings or to the demands of their research, the men are interested only in the movements of the woman's body. As the woman crosses her legs, accompanied by some light, Fellini-esque music, the men turn in unison and have their leers and grins captured forever in a freeze frame; she then unbuttons a button on her blouse, while the men crane their necks in an effort to glimpse her bra and breasts and once again get their expressions frozen. This use of freeze frames, then, helps capture the men's sleazy attitudes by exaggerating and preserving their unflattering expressions of lust.

This surreal scene does much more, then, than show us how close to civilization the children are. It also shows trained scientists rendered oblivious to the environment and to their jobs by their frustrated and warped preoccupation with sex. As such, the scene illustrates society's attitudes about sex and thus frames the girl's sexual fears and reluctance to deal with her sexual feelings. In an atmosphere like this, her hesitation is understandable.

As important as these scenes are, however, they seem just a preparation for the third use of freeze frames, the final confrontation between civilized man and primitive man. When the aborigine, the girl, and the boy find the abandoned house, the aborigine explores the land around it. While in the field, he sees a jeep and watches the driver indiscriminately gunning down countless animals. With each shot, herds of birds and animals flee. To document the futility of escape and defense, Roeg has the man kill a big water buffalo; as the animal falls, Roeg switches to an increasingly high grained film stock and to slow motion. Unlike the kangaroo sequence, however, here there is little dignity; death becomes instead ugly, painful, and final. To impress this upon us, Roeg follows with a closeup of the dead animal's head crawling with ants and maggots.

If this were not enough, Roeg repeats his technique of using a series of freeze frames. As the birds, animals, aborigine, and boy take flight from the carnage, each is momentarily frozen on the screen. The process of horror and escape are thus prolonged, emphasized, and engrained in our memories. Unlike the aborigine's killing of the kangaroo, which was almost peaceful, the white hunter's gun and mass killings cause deafening screams of terror and disorderly fleeing of wildlife from the entire area. As if in symbolic retaliation, an animal lunges at the young boy's feet, the first act of hostility by an animal towards the boy and his sister since they were thrust into the desert.

The freeze frames occur, then, three times. The first underscores the aborigine's harmonious relationship with nature; the second, the absurd and degrading sexual attitudes civilization inculcates in us; the third, the unnatural, total, and murderous effect civilization has on nature. We see nature first, then civilization, and then the inevitable but still horrifying confrontation between the two. Indeed, it is a confrontation that the good guy, if there is one, cannot win.

Walkabout, then, is more than a simple story about two children lost in the Australian desert and their adventures with a young aborigine. In addition, it is an intricately structured comment on the repressive power that modern society has over its people and on the unecological, monstrous capacity for mindless destruction that modern civilization exhibits. But unlike such a more political director as, for instance, Lina Wertmuller, Roeg does not seem interested in making us angry or disgusted enough to forge a new alternative. Instead, he cultivates a more omniscient, more wryly disinterested, and more ironically resigned reaction from the viewer.

As much perhaps as we should, we cannot get angry and politicized about the encroachment of civilization primarily because Roeg gives us no clear alternative to it other than the doomed and alien aborigine culture. We are shocked and saddened, of course, by the father's attack, the hunter's excesses, and the old man's inhumanity. Rather than capitalize on these events, however, Roeg mutes their horror by not dwelling on them and by moving on to and focusing on the children's adjustment to the events. We do not, for example, linger over the father's death scene; almost before we have a chance to assimilate it, the girl and boy are off into the desert; we quickly forget about the injustice and insanity of the father because we must worry about the children's immediate survival. And rather than being directed towards the environmental consequences of the hunter's destruction, we have to wonder about the aborigine's strange death; we do not have the luxury of thinking about the white hunter's actions because we have to cope with this new situation. Similarly, before we have a chance to get really angry with the old man for his sickening personality, we are thrust back to the city and to the girl's reverie. Even the final sequence mutes our response; Roeg does not end the movie with a strong political, social, or climactic note, but with a romanticized daydream, with the girl's wistful longing for the peace of nature and her lost youth. When we leave the theatre, then, we do not feel like blowing up the local butcher shop and retreating into the wilds and forging a new society. Instead, we are quietly depressed and filled with a yearning for a simpler time that is just like the girl's mood at the end of the picture.

To elicit this reaction from us, Roeg must prevent our prolonged identification with any one character. If, for example, we were to identify with the aborigine, we would be devastated by his death, at odds with the remainder of the film, and consumed by a desire for retribution. And if we were to identify totally with the girl, we would become too involved to appreciate the irony of the ending and would be inappropriately disgusted with the girl and with our own implied failure. To keep us more wryly disinterested and to insure our more objective perspective, Roeg, through his careful structure, keeps his characters dimensional. Although he places them in extraordinary situations, he never lets them assume heroic proportions, but keeps them human, with resulting faults, as well as strengths. In other words, he makes us care about them without making us wish we were them.

The young boy, for example, may be *Walkabout*'s most positive character. Although difficult in the beginning stages of the ordeal, he is likeable, intelligent, and adaptable, quickly developing a rapport with the aborigine and appreciating the adventure and beauty of the walkabout. But however admirable he is, he is still just a child; beyond his ability to adjust, he does not have that much to offer the adult audience. Rather than a fully developed character, he exists more as a contrast to the girl; his reactions, especially to the aborigine's dance and death, are pure, uncomplicated, and natural and thus allow us to see how the girl could have behaved had she not been so effectively socialized. Unfortunately, however, the boy's adaptability owes itself more to his youth than to anything else; as soon as he grows older, he undoubtedly will grow more rigid. Also, regardless of how the boy turns out, Roeg does not end the film with his response, but with the girl's. No matter how much we like the boy, he simply does not generate enough of an emotional attraction to engage us on a primal level; his final response becomes irrelevant to the film as it is now structured and is thus not missed.

The aborigine, who stands a better chance at becoming the film's hero, also remains relatively undeveloped. We know from his spontaneous, kind, and generous behavior that he is warm and compassionate. And to an urbanized viewer, his skill and compatability with the environment is awesome. When seen through his eyes, the brutal and wasteful devastation of the white hunter and the accompanying realization that the aborigine's way of life is doomed are heartbreaking. But, as he will later do with Newton in *The Man Who Fell to Earth*, Roeg never fully explains the aborigine. By

". . . from another, much different culture." In an exuberant mood, the aborigine hunts down a kangaroo.

treating him as a person from another, much different culture, Roeg prevents our understanding of and total identification with the aborigine.

Roeg undercuts our identification in large part just by not telling us why the aborigine commits suicide. Although we see him die and can think of at least four explanations for his death, our not knowing why makes any deep identification impossible.

Roeg's withholding of the reason for the suicide may prevent our identification with the aborigine (since we usually cannot identify with a character whose principal action remains a mystery), but does not stop us from wondering what the reason is. One theory suggests sexual motivation. The first time the girl and aborigine meet, the girl touches the aborigine's chest. The aborigine notices the touch; it may represent the first step of a sexual relationship that he is now prepared to define. This is why, the theory goes, the aborigine sends the boy on a frond-finding expedition, thus leaving him alone with the girl in the house, and why in the dance the aborigine keeps uncovering and covering his genitals. And since her behavior is so clearly sexually motivated, we could also expect the aborigine, who is the same age and on his rite of passage into manhood, to feel those same stirrings.

All of this is plausible, even probable. The theory is less success- ful, however, in dealing with the suicide. Because the girl rejects the aborigine's advances, the theory suggests, and because mating and death are so closely related in the life cycle and because her rejection represents a failure of sorts for the aborigine during his own walkabout, the substitution of death for sex is demanded.

Another explanation, suggested by the novel but unsupported by any specific evidence in the film is that on the walkabout, the aborigine is not allowed to frighten anyone. When the ritualistic dance frightens the girl, the aborigine must then kill himself. Al- though there is a contradiction in this theory, that he frightens the girl after he has started the dance, which seems like a dance of death, Roeg's refusal to define the dance makes this explanation possible, if not particularly plausible.

A similar but more convincing explanation depands upon the be- lief that by befriending and communicating with the white children, the aborigine broke a rule of the walkabout, which is a rigid ritual aimed at testing whether or not the boy can survive alone in the wilderness. Because the aborigine disobeys the rules, because he does not keep walking away from the two children at the oasis, he seals his fate. By showing them the road, the aborigine ends his responsibility and his usefulness to the children; he next has to fulfill his obligation to himself and his culture by killing himself.

Still another explanation revolves around the aborigine's witnessing of the hunter's mass and mechanized killing for sport. At this point, the aborigine sees progress, the upsetting of the balance of nature, and the eventual destruction of his and his family's way of life. The experience is understandably overwhelming; realizing he is soon to be rendered obsolete by the forces of history, the aborigine loses his will to live, lies down in the cow bones, paints a representation of a skeleton on his body, performs a dance of death ("his way of saying good-bye"), and kills himself.

Although all the theories could be true and the latter two seem especially believable, Roeg has kept any conclusive proof out of the movie. As a result, we cannot be exactly sure why the aborigine commits suicide. And while this lack of knowledge does not cause any trouble in the death of the father, which also remains unexplained, we are more involved with the aborigine and thus have a greater need to know why he died. But because we cannot know, we cannot fully understand the aborigine's final, most definitive action and cannot fully identify with him.

Even if we knew why he killed himself, however, the film is still structured around the girl, her reaction to his death, and her eventual re-entry into civilization. Because both she and we are products of modern civilization, because both are dealing with the same limited alternatives, and because both of us are uncertain about the cause behind the aborigine's suicide, we in the audience are placed in the same intellectual and, to some extent, emotional position she is in. But although this alliance should strenghten our emotional identification with the girl by giving us common situations, the ambiguity of his suicide, when coupled with her irritable, repressed behavior, sufficiently hinders any total identification we may have felt for her.

Although we immediately sympathize with the girl, who has just seen her father burn himself to death after failing to kill his children and who must now cope with her young brother and with the wilderness, her sexual repression and inability to adapt to her situation make her at times a very unattractive person. Her complaining, her failure to deal directly with the aborigine, and her imperialistic and hostile treatment of him at the farmhouse all give us reason to put a distance between her and us; hopefully, we think, we would never behave like that.

Even more damaging than her sexual fears and bad humor is the possibility that she may have helped cause the aborigine's suicide. That suspicion, which is fostered more by her refusal to confront her sexual feelings directly than by any specific interaction between the aborigine and the girl, undermines our response to her; we cannot help blaming or at least reserving judgment on her. As a result, we feel a deep-seated ambivalence towards her that makes any strong identification with her difficult.

Finally, we do not want to identify too closely with her because she wastes her chance for freedom. She holds herself back from the potential promise of the walkabout; her fears and caution, as well as her inability to trust her body and instincts, make her a negative role model, rather than a positive one. By the last scene, when we know her happy days cannot come again, we try to separate our fates from hers. Rather than behaving like her, we think, we would have made the most of such an opportunity. (Although, in reality, we may not have been able to do even as well as she did.)

To keep us further removed and objective, Roeg uses beautiful but extremely obtrusive cinematography and editing. When we are totally caught up in a movie, we are oblivious to any distinctions or obstacles existing between us and the film, including the theater, the audience, the photography, the editing devices. In *Walkabout*, however, dazzling superimpositions chronicle surreal parades of sunsets (which, although originally included to suggest the passage of time, function instead as the film's dominant visual image); freeze frames, slow motion, and film stocks of different grains are all used within a single scene.[1] Although truly beautiful, they are unavoidably noticeable. As we turn to the persons next to us to comment on their beauty, we are thrown out of the film and are reminded that what we are doing is watching a movie.

Rather than becoming one with the characters and living their experiences with them, we begin to watch the film from a distance; rather than becoming one with the film, we tend to be vicarious observers. Because we cannot become totally absorbed, we can operate not with anger or total gratification, but with that wry irony and cool omniscience that Roeg seems to be after. Nowhere is this better illustrated than in the story about the blind and dumb mother quoted at the beginning of this chapter.

It is a morbidly funny story, made funnier by the young boy's dramatic recitation of it. But what makes the story seem so important is the editing device Roeg develops for it. While the boy tells the story, Roeg cuts by turning pages. He pretends the frame is the page of the book; as the boy is talking, the entire frame is lifted up, revealing a new page with the boy, girl, and aborigine walking in a different place. It is as if we are reading the story, turning the pages of a moving, speaking picture book. Brilliant, original, and startling, this is editing that is guaranteed to draw attention to itself.

Now, a cryptic fable, especially when punctuated by a singular editing technique, often functions as the key to the entire movie, not unlike Borges' "The Man on the Mountain" fable from *Performance*. And, at first glance, the story seems to explain the movie with its talk of being stuck (although a remnant of *Performance*, here a suggestion of the girl's physical and mental situations), of being unable to communicate, and of being killed because of a broken neck. But despite its initial appearance as the key to the movie, the story turns out to be a smokescreen, funny in itself but of only limited application to the film's ambiguous issues.

The aborigine, who dies of a broken neck, must logically be the son on the windowsill, straining to hear what the woman is saying. And the girl, whose refusal to confront her own fears leads to her inability really to communicate with the aborigine, must be the mother, barricaded behind her door and talking only to herself. And, if the parable is correct, the boy, or the aborigine, dies because he wants to understand the girl and her ways.

Unfortunately, however, the story does not really tell us anything new. To function as the key to the movie, we would hope for a more specific, more exciting explanation. We already know that the aborigine's death has something to do with his experience with the white children; we do not need another affirmation of this generalization, but something more definitive, something not in the story.

Not only does it fail to tell us anything new, the anecdote's analogy to the film does not even survive strict scrutiny. According to the story, the boy wants to find out what the mother is talking about; but in the film, the aborigine never exhibits more than a cursory curiosity about the white children's toys or clothes and never intrudes on the girl's privacy, at least until the dance.

Although the story gives a superficial appearance of explaining the film, it merely teases us with some interesting connections and fails to reveal a single answer. Roeg, in fact, never even finishes the story. While we are laughing at the line about the broken neck, Roeg has the boy go on with the tale. "Well, his mother went on sitting there and talking to herself and she began to get worried because he was late home from work and his dinner would get spoiled. So she said—no, she didn't say anything. She got up and groped her way down the stairs. . . ." But before we can find out what happened, the children spot the red weather balloon and never get to finish the story. Thus, Roeg tantalizes and then frustrates and tricks us. He makes us work, fooling us into thinking that the more of his film we catch, the more answers we have. But instead, the more we work, the more we are sure that the answers are not there. Just as the girl cannot know why the aborigine dies, so must we be denied that information. And because we cannot know why he dies, we cannot exonerate the girl from the possible responsibility of his death and thus cannot hope to identify with her or any other character in the film.

In *Walkabout*, as in *Performance*, then, Roeg consciously removes us from the film. Even though *Walkabout*'s characters are more familiar and accessible than *Performance*'s, even though the three children go through a more basic, realistic, and believable ordeal, Roeg does not let us identify with the characters or their story. We cannot just have a good cry with them or sit on the edge of our seats, having our attention mindlessly pointed this way and that. Instead, we must be able to deal with the insecurity of not having heroes or explanations; we must be willing to use our own imaginations to adjust to its leisurely pace and to identify with Roeg's directorial omniscience and performance. And most of all, we must feel comfortable substituting an almost intellectual disinterest for our active involvement.

Because *Walkabout* asks us to do this, or at least works against our having a personal stake in the movie, it seems to me Roeg's least effective, least interesting, and least challenging movie. Although children, who are oblivious to the film's subtleties, are enthralled and excited by the adventure of the sister and brother, the alert adult witnesses a visually beautiful but somewhat trivial and almost academic discussion on civilization and its effects. And while the insistence on identification not with the characters or narrative of *Performance*, but with Roeg's intentions and design helped that movie, the rewards from *Walkabout*'s experience are not nearly so provocative; had we been made to feel more involved with the characters, especially with the girl, her final longing for the desert would seem much more poignant and much more important. Without that focus, we take little away from *Walkabout* than the memory of a series of beautiful pictures of the desert; by keeping us on his omniscient level, Roeg has made us understand his message, instead of feel his movie. It is a mistake he will not make in his next film, *Don't Look Now*.

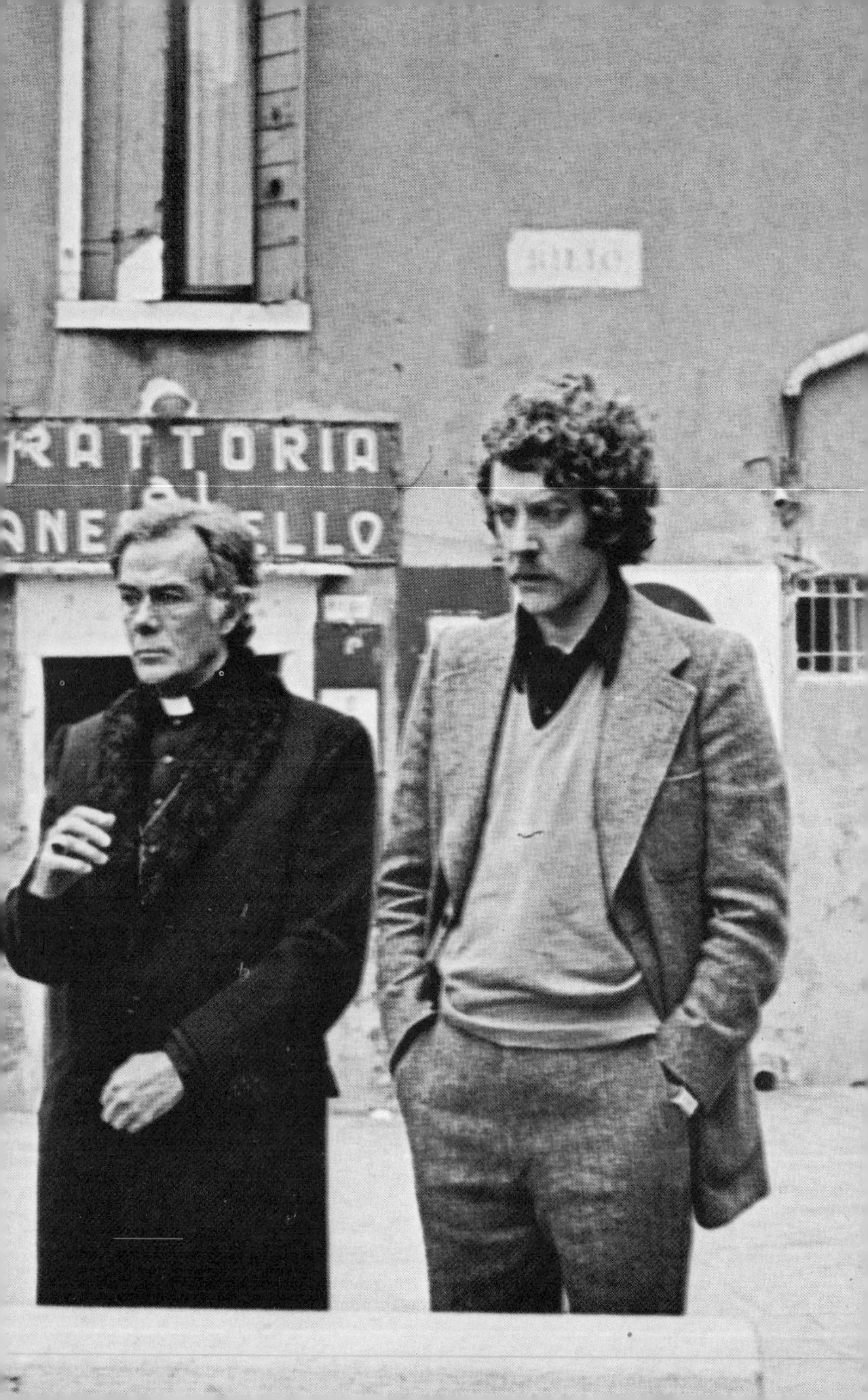
RATTORIA

4

Don't Look Now

"OSTRICHES . . . . LOST THE POWER OF FLIGHT a long time ago, before birds had developed into the many and different kinds we know. . . . Most flightless birds are leftovers from past ages. They are interesting but are less well adapted to life today."

Hunters know that ostriches run in circles when frightened and use this knowledge to kill or capture them.

It was hunted in Africa by Bushmen who disguised themselves in ostrich feathers. The hunter held up one arm to imitate the ostrich's head and neck. He moved in such an ostrich-like manner that he could come close enough to the birds to kill . . . . them with his bow and arrow.

Care is needed to keep ostriches and their relatives from becoming extinct (Herbert Zim, *Ostriches*).

* * *

"Ostriches do not bury their heads in the sand when they are frightened, as you may have heard. . . . But an old fable dies hard and this one is still being repeated although no ostrich has even been seen burying its head."

—*Zim's Ostriches*

* * *

"Nothing is what it seems."

—*Don't Look Now*

* * *

I

Don't Look Now testifies to Roeg's quickly emerging sense of control and discipline; while it covers similar ground to *Performance*, it is a much more focused, more accessible, and more emotionally effective movie. Not that it, too, does not make its own peculiar demands on the viewer.

It tells the story of a man who dies because he refuses to believe in the reality of non-rational, non-natural forces. If, like the charac-

The priest tells John he should have left Venice.

ter, we refuse to acknowledge the supernatural's existence, *Don't Look Now* seems unbelievable, contrived, and silly. If, on the other hand, we can accept this force as real, at least for the duration of the movie, if we can enter the movie on its own terms, then we will be swept into its relentless and terrifying progression of events.

If, then, we are willing to grant the existence of a supernatural power that makes ESP and fate credible, undeniable facts of life, the incidents in the film stop being convenient coincidences and become instead part of Roeg's careful and chilling design. And although we cannot consciously sort it out yet, the movie's opening sequence contains all the elements of that subliminal, supernatural design.

While looking at a slide of some stained glass windows in a church, John Baxter notices a red cloaked figure sitting in one of the church pews. Some glass falls from a window; John's son rides his bicycle over a mirror and breaks it; as if in response, John turns around, knocks over his drink, and causes the red color in the slide to run. At that moment, John's son, John Jr., checks his bicycle tire for glass fragments, cuts his finger on a sliver of glass, and bleeds. As both the boy and the slide bleed, Christine, John's daughter, chases after a red and white ball and falls into a pond. As the red color continues to spread over the slide and the screen, John dashes out of the house in an unsuccessful effort to save Christine. Through his editing, mise-en-scene, and coloration, Roeg quickly establishes John's clairovoyance (John has no other way of knowing Christine is in danger) and links together the glass, the red cloaked figure, and the two Johns. Roeg also isolates the less psychic Laura, John's wife and the children's mother. Unlike John, she does not sense the danger; she does not realize that something is wrong until she sees John carrying their dead daughter's body.

John's second sight is further demonstrated by his instinctive uneasiness over the two English sisters, Wendy and Heather, the blind psychic. When he notices them at the restaurant, he avoids their eyes and seems momentarily unsettled by their presence. Later, he objects to and is worried by Laura's increasing involvement with the two and their "mumbo jumbo." When Laura tells the women about John's hostility and reluctance even to meet them, Heather immediately understands. He is unwilling to acknowledge that he too has the gift of second sight, she explains, a gift that can be a "curse," as well as a gift.

Because such an admission would undermine the rational foundations John has built his life upon, he is intractable in his refusal to become friendly with the two sisters. But as much as he tries, he cannot prevent Laura from becoming involved with them. In one of their meetings, the women tell Laura that John is in great danger as long as he remains in Venice. When Laura tells him of the warning and begs him to leave, he refuses to take the warning seriously and makes a joke of it. Suddenly, however, he runs to the bathroom and vomits. "I haven't thrown up in ten years," he sheepishly admits later. The cause is obvious; he may not intellectually acknowledge his belief in the prophecy, but his psyche has been shaken by it.

John's continued efforts to shatter Laura's belief in the sisters' messages from their dead daughter further prove that he is troubled by the sisters and the implications of their warnings. Because of Heather's visions, Laura believes that Christine is happy; for the first time, Laura is able to accept the girl's death and find some solace. John, who later tells the police inspector that the women have given Laura what he has been unable to, tries to undermine Laura's faith in Heather's visions. "My daughter is dead! Dead! Dead!" he screams. "She does not come peeping from behind the fucking grave with messages for us." But like Chas's proclamation in *Performance* that he is a "man, a man all the time," John protests his disbelief too quickly and too intensely to be particularly convincing.

Thus, when the piece of wood falls through the scaffold and almost kills him, John is doubly upset. Not only has he almost lost his life, which would be understandably upsetting, but more importantly, he has had the warning confirmed that his life is in danger. "I was warned," he tells the bishop nervously. But, thinking that the accident has now canceled out the warning, John tries humorously to dismiss the prophecy of danger. To his and our surprise, however, the bishop refuses to laugh. "I wish I did not have to believe in prophecies, but I know too much not to," the bishop solemnly replies. John unfortunately does not listen to the threat behind the bishop's words; he quickly regains control of himself, reasserts his rational view of life, and shrugs off any further implications of the sisters' warning.

John's faith in the rationality of the world explains his ultimately fatal failure to call England immediately after seeing Laura, who is supposed to be in England with their injured son, on the Canal. Although Laura has far more reason to be in England than in Venice, John never doubts the validity of his sight; because he has seen her, she rationally and naturally has to be in Venice—despite his earlier observation that "nothing is what it seems." At any rate, since she is in Venice and has not called him, he reasons, she must be in the clutches of the two sisters. His certainty prevents him from performing the logical first step, from calling England and verifying or disproving her presence there, and causes him to spend all his efforts and time trying to find her in Venice. (Ironically, John does call the Venetian airport and finds out the plane left full but that there was no available passenger list. Had he then tried to call England, he would have discovered that the lines were down and that his phone call could not be completed. Roeg should have had him try to make the call; such an odd coincidence would support the film's atmosphere. At it now plays, John's failure to call England is just a little too unbelievable.)

Because John refuses to believe that Laura is not in Venice, he charges the two sisters with abduction and sets into motion the final chain of events that will lead to his death. That death will become increasingly frightening because of our increasing awareness of its inevitability and of the intricate and innocent actions that seal his fate. When John spills his drink on the slide, we realize that he is performing the first act in the chain of events that predetermine his death. And when John and Laura are at the restaurant and John closes the drafty window, he causes another window to pop open and send a gust of wind into the room. A particle of dust lodges in Wendy's eye, providing the opportunity for the sisters to stop staring and start talking to Laura. Through an innocent action on John's part, then, the movie is propelled forward and John moves one step closer to his death.

Thus, be they innocent or not, the two sisters are obviously implicated in John's fate. They reveal Christine's presence to Laura and draw Laura into the realm of the supernatural. After the meeting in the restaurant, the sisters are rarely far from Laura or John, mysteriously appearing at a church where Laura impulsively stops to pray (at the same church that is in the slide at the beginning of the movie) and at the church that John is restoring. Even more sinisterly, they will also be outside the police inspector's window when John is talking about them.

Even more unsettling than their actual physical presence and Heather's haunting, unseeing gaze are two cheat shots that Roeg uses. When Laura is trying to convince John that the sisters mean them no harm, Roeg shows us the two women laughing hysterically. Although we do not know what they are laughing about, the implication that they represent danger and evil for Laura and John is unmistakable. The second shot is even more damaging. When John climbs up the scaffold, one of the oval reflections of light captured by the camera turns into a mirror. (And we remember from *Performance* the significance of mirrors.) Wendy's face, again laughing, appears in the mirror. Since the next shot is of the wood falling through the scaffold and almost killing John, we must feel that Wendy either caused or knew about the accident. When coupled with their mysterious habit of being in the same place as Laura and John, we have no choice but to share John's fears about their motives and actions.

Once we become suspicious, additional coincidences intensify our feelings of distrust and fear. The sisters move from their cramped, somewhat seedy pensione to a much fancier hotel—on the very morning that John needs to find them. Had they stayed, John would have realized that Laura was not in Venice and thus could have averted his encounter with the red-cloaked murderer. Because their original hotel room was so dingy, we could normally accept their move; the suddenness and coincidence of the move, when coupled with our suspicions about their motives and roles, however, imbues it with more ominous implications.

Even more interesting is that Wendy, the non-blind sister, returns to her new hotel room before Heather and John. We know that Heather and John leave the police station for the hotel well before Wendy even gets back to the station, that Heather is exhausted and wants to go straight to the hotel, that Heather finds Venice especially suited to blind people because she can walk so well there, and that the new hotel seems to be in an inland part of Venice, accessible primarily by foot, not by vaporetto. Yet, when John and Heather arrive at the hotel, Wendy is in the room waiting for them. Although not conclusive, Wendy's improbably early arrival at the hotel feeds our suspicion that the two sisters are leading or at least helping John into a trap.

Also strange is Wendy's insistence that Laura come up to see Heather, only to have Heather send her back to the street in search of John. Wendy knows how serious the situation is; surely she could have told Laura herself. And when Heather talks to Laura, she ends by taunting her. "We told you he was in danger; we told you to get him out of Venice; we told you and you didn't listen."

Rather than acting hysterical or concerned, Heather appears instead to be mocking Laura. This exchange, which in retrospect seems entirely unnecessary, takes up an unfortunate amount of time; had Wendy sent Laura off immediately, Laura could have found him before he ran into the building and could thus have conceivably prevented John's confrontation with the dwarf. Once more, then, an interlocking set of coincidences advance John's movement towards his death.

Ultimately, the sisters seem unavoidably malevolent. While we cannot accuse them of causing John's death, their laughter and their participation in the chain of events that leads John to their hotel room and to the murderer at the very least implicate them as a part of the web that throws John and the murderer together.

Although not in Roeg's original conception of the movie, the police inspector works in the same way.[1] The first time he sees John and Laura is when Laura is being taken to the hospital. The inspector is on a bridge, dredging for the body of a murder victim, but stops to stare at John and Laura. The next time we see him is in his office. As John confides in him about his fears for Laura's safety and his concern for her mental condition, the inspector doodles on the police artist's sketches of Wendy and Heather, drawing eyes on the blank spaces of the blind sister's sockets. He seems to know what John is saying even before John says it; as he stares out the window, he sees Wendy and Heather walk by his office. While they are too far away for the inspector to make a positive identification, Heather's blindness seems apparent, even at that distance. Although he probably should not be expected to pick the two women up immediately, the coincidence of their appearance, when seen against the inspector's strange, almost indifferent, and preoccupied manner ("the job of the police artist," he distractedly mutters at one point, "is to make the living appear dead") and his failure even to notice the women all make him suspect.

Even more curious is the inspector's failure to suggest to John, who is obviously upset and unable to think clearly, that he call England. While John does not question his own rationality, his behavior gives the police inspector every reason to do so; he should be expected to provide John with this most logical of suggestions. More strange than that is his having Laura met at the airport and then bringing her back to the police station. Since he sees John and Heather leave for the hotel, he could have easily had her escort take her directly there. Instead, he has her brought back to the station, where all he does is give her directions to the hotel. Since this provides a delay that sends John out on the streets alone and to his death, the action seems unusual and unfortunate. Especially when seen with his failure to take a more active role in the investigation and with his threatening personality, the delay indicates his general compliance, be it intentional or accidental, with the sisters and with the events that culminate in John's death.

The bishop is another character who seems somehow, although less actively, involved with John's fate. A very serious man who, John thinks, would "make God feel slightly less than immaculate," the bishop is acutely aware of the existence of an evil force that rivals God's and that is beyond man's rational comprehension. Perhaps because he does not give an "ecclesiastical fuck" about the restoration of the church's artwork and is more concerned about God's "priorities," we realize that the bishop is aware of the potential danger that John is in. He tells John to take the prophecies seriously; when he later says that John should have left Venice with Laura, we realize that he is right and that John will soon die. When John leaves the sisters' room to follow the figure in red, the bishop is jolted awake. He turns on the light and then turns it off again. As he lies back down, the camera moves in on the room's most noticeable adornment, a red glass with a candle in it. As we watch, the candle flickers, and goes out. Shortly thereafter, as John is bleeding to death, the bishop reawakens, suggesting that he too has the second sight and knows what is happening to John. Even worse, yet consistent with the bishop's personality, is his inability to do anything about it; although aware of the gravity of John's situation, he has been unable to help John in any way.

The bishop is tied to the sisters and to the film's events visually as well as thematically. Wendy wears a semi-circular gold broach with three globes hanging from it. The camera emphasizes the piece just before Wendy bumps into Laura in the restaurant; Laura notices it when she goes to the sisters' first hotel room. The shape reappears on the mosaic that John is restoring; the rest of the face of the original design has worn away, leaving only the shape. While trying to restore the face, which will alter the shape, John is almost killed. Later, the shape will reappear, although in a more elongated form, as an icon on the bishop's office wall. At the end of the movie, John's blood will coagulate into the same shape. And, through a flashback to the introductory montage, we realize that the shape was introduced when the slide bled the same way at the beginning of the film. Thus, the shape seems just one more indication that all the characters, including the ineffectual but distraught bishop, are linked together, that no one is innocent or removed from John's death.

However interesting and involved these characters are, their shifty eyes, shady appearances, and sinister and troubled countenances make them familiar, almost conventional components of the horror film. What distinguishes *Don't Look Now*, what makes it even more terrifying, are the roles John and his own family play.

John and Laura, along with McCabe and Mrs. Miller, are perhaps the most dimensional, likeable, and human couples in contemporary movies, maybe because although deeply in love, each retains his or her individuality. That John and Laura love each other is apparent; the private looks, the respect, the concern for each other, and the depth of feeling captured in the love scene make their love obvious. To keep the relationship from getting cloying, Roeg hints at their problems; John sometimes shuts Laura out because of his work, as he does in the restaurant, and resents the sisters making her happy, which he feels is his job; Laura at times tries to blame John for their daughter's death. Still, these are just by-products of two people living together; without these little flaws, they would seem far too idealized.

Even though they love each other deeply, they remain two people. In the love scene, for instance, the music, pacing, and emotion between the two remove any hint of vulgarity from the scene; despite its explicitness (even in the edited American version), the feelings generated by the two make it a love scene, not a sex scene. Despite this distinction, however, the scene's time sequence is jumbled; by the end of it, the two do not end up as one, entwined in each other's arms, but instead as two very satisfied, very loving, but very distinct individuals.

This becomes important because even though Laura's love for John does not have to be questioned, she too not only fails to save him, but pushes forward the events leading to his death. Although, for instance, she readily accepts and finds peace from Christine's post-death visits, she forgets the warning about John's being in danger as long as he is in Venice. After faking a relapse of her mental breakdown so that he will agree to leave Venice, she relaxes her guard. Thus, when the call from England comes, she reacts instinctively—by taking the first plane out of Venice and leaving John alone there. Her panic and need to be near her only surviving child are understandable. Still, she should have made John, who is in greater danger, go in her place. But instead she goes, permitting John to have his vision of her, the vision that, more than anything else, propels him towards his death.

Laura's complicity in the film's events works at a more subtle, more frightening level as well. "As women grow older," the police inspector says, "they look more and more like each other; they converge." And although less dramatically than in *Performance, Don't Look Now* also deals with the converging of identities; by the end of the film, Laura, Wendy, and Heather are united in a strong bond that both excludes John and depends upon his death. John himself admits that the two sisters have given a peace and happiness to Laura that he has been unable to provide. Indeed, from the beginning, the three women have responded in an instinctive, almost psychic way. Once they have met, John can do nothing to keep them apart. Because we trust and like John so much more than the two sisters, we share his unease at Laura's increasing involvement with them; we sense that John and Laura are moving apart while Laura and the sisters are becoming increasingly intertwined.

We are not especially surprised, then, when the funeral boat passes and reveals Laura flanked by the two women. It is as if the women have endured; the two sisters will be there to support Laura psychologically. Their presence may explain Laura's expression on the funeral boat. When Christine dies, Laura becomes hysterical; for John's death, she is more controlled, serene, and statuesque. Her final facial expression, surprisingly, is a smile.

That smile may be used as proof not just that the women have converged, but that the convergence is of a malevolent nature, that the women, especially the sisters, have succeeded in eliminating John. Because John's death frees Laura from a conflicting relationship, she is now able to enter the world of women; his death becomes, then, a liberating experience that causes her to smile.

Another, less fantastic interpretation of the smile rests upon Laura's acceptance of Christine's death; her belief that Christine is happy and still very much with her gives Laura great comfort.

Similarly, even though John has died, he too will always be with her. He may no longer be a physical presence in her life, but his continued psychic existence contributes to her new self-sufficiency and serenity.

Both interpreatations raise questions. The first seems too strong and too pat to be totally convincing; the second too neatly minimizes the terror of John's death and the atmosphere of the entire film. Without a definitive meaning from Roeg, however, the smile remains ambiguous; one time, it may seem a moving and courageous gesture; another time, it may seem chilling and evil. In either case, however, the smile is evidence of Laura's ability to survive without John and acts as a confirmation that she too has helped advance the chain of events.

Fate or whatever name we choose to call the force operating on John is strong enough to include even John and Laura's children, including the dead daughter, Christine. Although Christine tries through Heather to warn John about the danger Venice poses, the vision of her red raincoat continually leads John through Venice's streets. But while John feels he is chasing his dead daughter, he is actually chasing the dwarf in the red cloak. And, in the film's final moments, as the vision of Christine turns into the murderous and aged dwarf, Roeg devastatingly converges the two females; the extremes of the age spectrum are twisted together and united by the merging of the very young girl and the ancient woman. Even though she is dead, then, Christine too complies with the process of John's death; even she is involved.

John, Jr. is also an agent of his father's death. His minor injury is especially convenient since it happens as soon as John agrees to leave Venice. Before Laura can get him out of Venice, however, John, Jr. gets hurt and provides the excuse to get Laura, not John, out of Venice. When John is stabbed, John, Jr., like the bishop, wakes up; he too knows that something extraordinary is happening. And finally, when on the funeral boat, John, Jr. can be identified not by his features, which we cannot make out, but by his bright red cap. As we shall soon see, the color red will tie the entire film together. For now, though, his wearing of the red cap, his waking up in the night, and the timing of his accident are enough to implicate him too in his father's death.

Even though the peripheral characters and members of John's family must assume responsibility for John's death, John not only does little to save himself, but also, more than any other single character, sets the events in motion. On the most basic level, he spills the drink on the slide and causes it to bleed and opens the restaurant window, giving the sisters their opportunity to make contact. More important, he repeatedly refuses to acknowledge his second sight, to heed the warnings, and to readjust his priorities away from the rational, tangible realities of the church restoration project to the more immediate, more frightening psychic demands. When in the restaurant, for instance, he chooses his work, the slides, over his concern for Laura, who has been almost comatose in the rest room for hours. Because he cannot face the existence of an afterlife, he continually tries to undermine Laura's belief in it, even though this belief is enabling her finally to cope with Christine's death and with her life. And although he may be partially motivated by his concern for Laura, he is also motivated by envy; the two sisters are providing something he has not been able to give Laura himself.

He also, of course, refuses to heed any warnings he has been given. And, most importantly, he refuses to accept the fact that his vision of Laura on the canal in, had he stopped to analyze what he saw, a funeral boat, could be a manifestation of his second sight. But instead, he takes it as evidence that she is still in Venice; then, when this proves false, he dismisses the vision from his mind entirely, even though this is the clearest warning of all.

Thus, despite repeated warnings from Christine, Laura, the sisters, the bishop, and his own clairvoyance, John refuses to acknowledge what is happening. Instead of listening and evaluating the events, John continues to act as if nothing were unusual and threatening. Because of this arrogance and provincial insistence on a rational, empirical interpretation of events, he, more than anyone else, makes his death the inevitable climax of the movie.

Still, although John sets the events of the movie in motion, he cannot be thought of as guilty or suicidal, just cavalier, unlucky, and doomed. Throughout the movie, ominous touches like candles going out to the accompaniment of spooky organ music and the flash forward/vision of Laura on the canal prepare us for John's death. That it is preordained is underscored by the montage of the death scene, which recalls and explains the opening montage. We see that when John is knifed by the dwarf, he falls. In the fall, he kicks out some glass from a window. This glass is the same glass that falls and lands under John, Jr.'s bicycle. Because time and space can be totally malleable in the movies, one of John's final actions relates to one of the film's earliest; even if we do not find out exactly how or why until much later, the events of the film seem intertwined and preordained from the beginning. And, as the final montage makes clear, everyone, from Laura, the children, the bishop, the sisters, the dwarf, to John himself, merely play out their roles.

For this reason, *Don't Look Now* cannot end any other way; it is totally structured around the existence of a malevolent, inescapable, and indefinable force bearing down on John. Its presence and the complicity it demands from the other characters make everyone seem to be telling less than they know or to be acting on unrevealed, unconscious, or sinister motives. And although John refuses to acknowledge the force's existence, he is certainly unable to ignore, outrun, or beat it.

Ultimately, then, the terror does not stem from the sudden appearance of that horrible and wrinkled dwarf or from the slow, ugly way John has to die. Instead, we are frightened because a part of us, perhaps more primitive than our rational and intellectual faculties, realizes that yes, there may be such a power controlling our own fates. As such, *Don't Look Now* becomes, as Freud describes, "that class of the terrifying which leads us back to something long ago known to us, once very familiar." Or, as Tobe Hooper, director of the cult film, *The Texas Chain Saw Massacre*, explains the true horror film: "The idea is to establish a context that personifies the death angel. . . . A pistol is as lethal as a ghost or a ghoul, but a ghost or ghoul scares us more. . . . for a pistol [to be] a frightening device, it needs to somehow represent the Grim Reaper, that dark, unknown force that is even more frightening than termination. . . . The notion of the angel that ends it all and then takes us through the vapor to an unknown area is the real terror."[2]

Which is precisely what Roeg has done in *Don't Look Now*; even before he plunges us into the mists of the last scene, he has made an adult horror movie about these powers of darkness. And since we have spent two hours watching John die primarily because he has refused to admit that these powers exist, we have a very convincing reason not to make that same mistake ourselves.

Traditionally, the powers of darkness and our fear of them are tempered by the powers of light; the good or benevolent balances or even defeats the evil. In *Don't Look Now*, however, the powers of light, as represented by conventional Christian symbols, are depicted as ineffectual and empty. The film opens, for example, with a shot of a shimmering cross made by rain falling on a pond. In moments, Christine will die on that same spot. Later, the cross will reappear in Venice, only to be dispelled by a housewife throwing dirty water on it. As soon as the cross disappears, the dwarf appears and begins to lead John into the maze of Venice's interior. Thus, Christine and the dwarf are tied together visually through the cross. Rather than bringing peace or salvation, however, the cross seems to accompany, but to be incapable of preventing, tragedy.

The additional Christian symbolism is equally ineffective. Much of the movie takes place in unused, decaying churches; religious icons are broken and eroded; crosses are discussed for their artistic or historical value. In all cases, they have become empty and powerless symbols of an ineffective and fragmented faith, incapable of offering solace or reassurance. Even the most prominent religious symbol, the bishop, has lost faith in the powers of good; rather than working to impose God's will, he spends his time worrying about the apparent triumph or at least ascendance of the powers of evil.

Now, in today's secular world, the comment that the trappings of organized religion do not have much meaning is almost a cliché. What distinguishes *Don't Look Now* is not, then, its skeptical outlook on the church and the benevolence of the universe, but the skill Roeg uses in making us believe in the power of the supernatural. Without this belief, the movie would seem a superficial, non-suspenseful (the flash foward tells us how it will end), but beautifully photographed story of a murder. If we believe, however, we are thrust into John's threatening, inexplicable encounter with the supernatural, non-rational world.

Roeg does so without the gimmickry of *The Exorcist*, the theatrical intellectualizations of Bergman, or most of the campy conventions of the "B" horror movies. Instead, he relies on the creation of a magnificently unsettling and eerie atmosphere and on an apparently tangible and "real" mass murderer. Under Roeg's eye, Venice in the off season becomes an impenetrable series of mazes and misty streets, devoid of any life. In addition to Nino Rota's wistful, poignant neo-classical music, Roeg uses discordant noise and electronic sounds that substitute for the more normal and reassuring sounds of

John restores a dwarf-like gargoyle.

street life and traffic. He also includes ghostly cries and moans, usually linked to the dwarf and Christine and used while John is being lured deeper and deeper into the city.

In addition to the visual and aural devices that make us uneasy, the constant ambiguity of the characters' motives help create feelings of loneliness, danger, conspiracy. The bishop, the police inspector, the sisters, when placed within the atmosphere of the film, all seem to know what is happening to John. More than his specific actions almost, the inspector's eyes and expressions implicate him in his dealings with John; if we were to meet him on the street, we would instinctively want to avoid him. By not explaining the sisters' laughing and the bishop's reluctance and inability to help, Roeg intensifies our suspicions and makes us worried, frustrated, and tense. And the repeated, hideous, and sobering shots of Christine drowning, the blind woman's eyes, the dead body in the canal, and the decaying state of Venice itself consolidate and amplify our uneasy reactions.

These atmospheric details are given even more focus by the very real threat of the mass murderer. We see the red cloaked figure run out of a house where a woman is screaming and crying for help. Because we have seen two searches for the murder victims' bodies, we easily connect the dwarf with the murders. We also hear John worrying about Laura's safety while the murderer is loose. When John finally confronts and is killed by the dwarf, she is not a nebulous, amorphous super-natural force, but a bizarrely ugly human being. Because we know, then, that there is an actual murderer afoot, John's death becomes grounded to a believable, naturalistic reality, a reality that makes the atmosphere surrounding it that much more real, that much more frightening.

Although some critics, Charles Champlin in particular, have criticized Roeg for trying to play the film both ways by giving the murderer such a "real" form, Roeg's decision to ground one foot in the natural order and the other in the supernatural gives the film a much needed credibility.[3] Had we been asked to believe that John is mysteriously killed by an unnamed, unseen force, our reaction would have been diffused. By seeing the dwarf, whom we recognize as the murderer, actually kill John, Roeg is able to give us in concrete form the agent of John's death, or, as Hooper would call her, the death angel—without sacrificing the more ominous, more ambiguous, and more frightening supernatural overtones. Her actual identity, be she a maniacal old woman or the grim reaper, becomes almost irrelevant; what assumes more importance is that her action confirms the prophecy and concludes the process of John's death. While we are startled and horrified by the dwarf's sudden appearance, we are much more unsettled by our ability finally to see how smoothly everything and everyone in John's universe, including John himself, cooperated, even conspired, to push the events forward. We can see, in other words, how John's fate takes him into that unknown area Hooper talks about; we can feel the terror begin.

II

One look at *Performance* is enough to remind us how controlled Roeg has become. Although both *Performance* and *Don't Look Now* depend upon our ability to react to non-rational, non-naturalistic modes of reality, *Don't Look Now* is much more focused and single-minded. Because it lacks *Performance*'s metaphysical confusion, literary ambitions and allusions, and psychedelic and unrestrained photography and because it offers more conventional and identifiable characters, *Don't Look Now* is a much more accessible movie. Even on the first viewing, then, we know what is happening.

The basic difference in the two films can be illustrated by the ways each uses the color red. In both, red is a recurring visual motif. In *Performance*, Chas's first lover puts a red dot on her face. Later, we see the red paint, the red room, the red dye, the red lips, the red mushroom, the red screen, the red blood. Although we sense that it connects everyone and has something to do with the identity transference, the red does not play a large or specific enough role to really work effectively; instead, it becomes just one more noticeable component with which we must work to tie the film together. And because it is only one of many components that need to be integrated into each other, it tends to be a loose end or at best a visual device that must be consciously linked to all the others in the puzzle before it can have much impact.

In *Don't Look Now*, however, the color red serves as the film's unifying force, linking the world of the dead, Christine, to the world of the living. The red in the dwarf's cloak bleeds and stains the slide and frame; Christine wears a red raincoat and drowns while chasing a red and white ball, a ball that Laura will hide in her suitcase and always keep close to her. The Italian child in the hospital that responds so well to Laura plays with the same type of red ball.

Heather convinces Laura that Christine really was sitting at the restaurant table only by describing the red coat of Christine's; whenever we see the dwarf, we really see just the red cloak she wears or the blur of red darting in and out of doorways. The bishop has a red candle-glow to his room; Laura in the final shots is framed by bright red geraniums in the black funeral boat; John, Jr. is recognizable only because he is wearing a bright red cap. St. Nicolaus, in addition to being the patron saint of the church that John is restoring (and Roeg's first name), is identified with Laura, who is also "kind to children and animals," and is also the address of the sisters' second hotel room. St. Nick is also, of course, characterized by the red Santa costume. Red, the color of blood, passion, and violence, seems an appropriate color for the characters and the film to share, a color typifying the unknown, the dangerous, the non-rational, the emotional.

The red does not, however, become a conventional literary symbol in the way, say, that the mirrors in *Performance* do. The mirrors, although *Performance*'s most important recuring visual pattern, still must be explained verbally by Pherber as the link with the loss of Turner's demon. Given this information, we are thus able to deal with the mirrors.

Roeg does not do that in *Don't Look Now*; rather than have the red "mean" anything in an analytical way, he uses it to establish a purely visual consistency that links his characters and story. Thus, we follow John as he chases the red, catches it, and is killed by it. Hooper, although still describing his own *Texas Chain Saw Massacre*, explains best how the red works: "I build and construct [the film] in such a way that it's a mathematical method not just in the rhythm of the cutting, but in the content of what you see, what you feel, and when you feel it. About halfway through a show, or even earlier, the accumulation of and the way the images have been presented begin to open little trap doors in the mind . . . . there are messages . . . . And when all these things accumulate at the moment of impact, they make the impact powerful . . . . and pure."[4] In other words, the red goes beyond an intellectual function; it becomes an almost subconscious, subliminal presence that consolidates and heightens our reaction to the film.

To focus our attention further, Roeg also eliminates much of *Performance*'s self-indulgence and self-conscious decadence. In place of Turner and Chas, who were always kept at a distance from us, Roeg gives us two upper-middle class, educated, dynamic, and attractive people involved in a positive, loving, heterosexual relationship. Because of John and Laura's warmth, physicality, decency, and maturity, we immediately care about them. Unlike our ambivalent feelings towards Chas and Turner and our ultimate identification in *Performance* with Roeg, here we identify with John and Laura. And that identification contributes to our more direct and more emotional response to *Don't Look Now*.

Roeg maximizes this reaction by using his most restrained and most functional cinematography to date. Again unlike *Performance* with its extreme camera angles, characters turning green, and mountains turning into breasts, *Don't Look Now*, although stunning to watch, is discrete enough to blend the visuals into the film's larger design. Rather than distract us by the beauty of an individual shot, Roeg keeps the images flowing into each other, rarely letting them draw attention to themselves. In this way, he keeps us inside the movie; because we are not drawn out of the film by startling visuals, we are forced to identify with the characters even more.

Even Roeg's use of squeeze motion and discontinuous, non-naturalistic editing is directed towards our continued identification with the characters. As in *Walkabout*'s suicide scene in which the father falls to the ground several times, Roeg's editing of John's coming out of the water is composed of three cuts; in the first, John emerges from the water, throws his head back, and begins to scream; suddenly Roeg cuts back to him still coming out of the water—in other words, Roeg repeats a part of the previous shot. The second cut ends with John throwing his head back in pain; the third shot begins with John beginning to throw his head back, once more repeating part of the sequence. In addition to the scene's disjointed editing and the filming of it in slow motion, Roeg throws the sound out of sync. When John screams, the sound is not immediately picked up; his mouth opens well before we hear the sound.

Although the scene is filmed non-naturalistically, the sequence is not only a creative and powerful presentation of the drowning, but is also a surprisingly realistic portrayal of the way we actually see during crisis situations. "I saw it coming in slow motion," we often say when talking about an accident, a fall, or a winning pass; in moments like these, our normal frame of vision and time is disrupted to the point that time stops or changes. In fact, novelist

Sterling Watson, who saved his daughter from a drowning similar to Christine's, says that the drowning scene in the movie was so much like the way he saw and functioned in his own crisis that he could not bear to watch the movie and had to leave the theater. So, when the beam falls onto the scaffold in slow motion and when Laura faints and the food and dishes spill over her for such an extended period of time, we are not distracted by the artificiality or artistic virtuosity of the sequence because that is the way we would see them in our everyday lives. Oddly enough, then, when *Don't Look Now* uses its time most fluidly and when it should look the least natural, Roeg has actually achieved a terrifyingly heightened sense of realism. Rather than being thrown out of the movie, we are continually strapped in.

The narrative also facilitates our involvement in the story and characters. Unlike *Performance*'s jumpy and confusing plot, *Don't Look Now* does not keep us in the dark very often. With the exception of the beginning montage, whose subtleties are obscured by the horror of Christine's death, the concluding montage, which pulls everyone together in John's death, and the clearly defined flashforward, the plot moves smoothly from one related event to the next. Although we may not know why events are happening, we almost always know what is happening.

The most famous and pivotal scene in the film, the truncated love scene, is the only one that does not fit the pattern of clearly defined, linear development. In it, Roeg intercuts Laura and John's lovemaking with their getting dressed afterwards and preparing to go out. They will, for example, be kissing each other and rolling over; on the turn, however, Roeg will cut to a fully dressed Laura putting her lipstick on. Then it is back to bed, where the couple will be locked in a still passionate embrace. Accompanied by a haunting and fragile melody, the love scene cannot really be described; its beauty, emotions, and eroticism go beyond the powers of language.

Although breaking up their lovemaking with shots of their individual post-intercourse activities sounds as though Roeg is commenting on their alienation from each other, it instead enables him to document how they function both as a unit and as two separate individuals. The satisfaction they derive and the respect that they feel for each other are evident by the ways they look at each other, treat each other, and make us respond to them. They are also, however, secure enough to maintain two individual identities; they do not have to deny their individuality in a frantic and ultimately fruitless effort to become one.

The love scene also serves as a divider and bridge between the two parts of the movie. In the first part, we concern ourselves mostly with Laura. Her scream transports us from England and the film's introduction to Venice; in this early part of the film, we watch her cope with Christine's death, get increasingly involved with the two sisters and the occult, and begin to fear Venice. While John probes, questions, and worries, he seems to be reacting to Laura's emotional condition, rather than initiating any action of his own. Because Laura is at this point more dynamic, we respond more strongly to her than to John, who is little more than the concerned husband. But after the love scene, which is visually distinct from the rest of the movie because of its extended manipulation of time, the movie will become John's. In the very next scene, he will get them lost, leaving Laura to react and find their way through Venice. Then, just as she convinces him to leave Venice, the phone call from England comes. She leaves Venice instead of John and no longer plays an active role in the film; except for the flash-forward and the telephone conversation, we do not even see her again until the end of the film.

Since John and Laura change roles, since John will become the primary actor and our main focus, Roeg must give us some indication of the switch. The love scene, which involves a physical transfer of energy, seems the perfect place for such a transfer to occur. To catch the fleeting physical pleasure of their love, Roeg takes the entire episode, from the beginning of their lovemaking to their leaving the hotel, and carefully shuffles the sequence of events. As he rearranges the individual moments, he rearranges Laura and John's roles as well. Had the two just made love and left the hotel, only the plot would have prepared us for the shift of emphasis from Laura to John as the person in danger. By mixing the time sequence of the love scene, however, Roeg visually announces the transfer. As we go into the love scene, Laura is the one who has been occupying most of our attention and moving the events. After we leave the scene, however, that role passes to John. Because Roeg is upsetting our identification process and switching our focus, the love scene, with its juxtaposition of natural time and sequence, gives him a chance to effect the transfer visually. Theme and technique are masterfully intertwined; we go in expecting a straight-forward sex scene but find instead the sex cut with its aftermath. We go in, then, with Laura as the actor and John the reactor and leave with those roles reversed.

The intercutting enhances the love scene in another way as well, by capturing the impermanence and elusiveness of physical pleasure. At each point in the scene, we are aware of the encounter's end. Thus, we are constantly being reminded of how finite and temporary John and Laura's passion is. Because it cannot last forever, their lovemaking becomes that much more precious and poignant—because we are constantly reminded of its end, we better appreciate the beauty of the moment.

The flash-forward serves the same purpose; as soon as John sees Laura on the funeral boat, we know he must die. Because the horror of this film does not stem from whether or not John dies but instead from the process of his death, the flash-forward does not detract from the film's suspense. On the other hand, it makes us want John to live that much more. When we are made aware of his imminent death, we realize how valuable life is. As soon as John's death becomes inevitable, our emotional involvement with him and our desire to see him live are sharpened. And when the end comes, we suffer an increased shock and sadness, for we have a much greater sense of what John and, by implication, what we have lost.

Unlike *Performance*, then, which rambles and deals intellectually with elusive and demanding concepts, *Don't Look Now* is a direct, emotional, and somewhat single-minded movie. Like all the Roeg films, it has an unparalleled visual beauty and grasp of atmosphere, as well as the integrity to tell its story visually, rather than verbally. And to the alert and flexible viewer, it has an irresistible power and impact.

To the causal film-goer or to the more traditional film critic who insists upon a literary, rational, or naturalistic framework, however, *Don't Look Now* more often seems aimless, boring, overblown, confusing. The movie's relatively poor performance at the box office and the flurry of disparaging reviews from some of the major critics prove that there are more traditional viewers than adventurous ones. That Venice, Julie Christie, a hot sex scene, and a Christmas release date were not enough to make this a big financial success all suggest that Roeg is not and may never be a commercial director—this was to be, after all, his simple "yarn" picture.[5] Not that *Don't Look Now's* failure to make millions seemed to bother Roeg much; after finishing it, he began work on his most ambitious project, *The Man Who Fell to Earth*.

5

The Man Who Fell to Earth

"I REMEMBER WHEN MOMMA used to put us on a train. I was about ten and we'ld go to Oklahoma City to visit Granny. Then, about six years later, the concession stands were gone; there weren't too many people on the train; there weren't any dining cars and the seats were all shabby. It's a shame; I used to like trains."

(—from *The Man Who Fell to Earth*)

* * *

"A year after *The Man Who Fell to Earth* was released in the United States, the producer finally found a distributor for the movie in France. Its star, David Bowie, attended the premiere as a break from working on Iggy Pop's new album in Berlin. Escorting model Synde Rome, Bowie was almost choked when a fan grabbed his scarf and wouldn't let go as Bowie made his way into the theater. Bowie graciously gave the scarf to the fan when he finally freed himself. He was less gracious a few seconds later when another fan grabbed for his wallet. Bowie grabbed it back, socked the guy—breaking his own thumb in the process—and ran inside." (*Rolling Stone*'s "Random Notes")[1]

* * *

"That company that makes the self-developing film I showed you a while ago, they made this announcement there. They're dumping computers and installing human beings. You want to know why? They want to bring back human errors because that's the way you get new ideas. By making mistakes. Back to man. His imagination."

Although Professor Bryce is speaking about World Enterprises, Newton's company in *The Man Who Fell to Earth*, he could just as well be talking about the film itself. For instead of making an ordinary movie, Roeg has tried in his fourth film to take more chances and to attempt more than would normally be thought possible.

105

The end—not with a bang, but a whimper.

Scriptwriter Paul Mayersberg describes the film's ambitions in lofty, even pretentious terms: "One of [Roeg's] primary interests in film was as a time machine. He was referring to the fact that you can move the film and the characters back and forth, especially during the process of editing. You can even go sideways, guessing as it were, at a state that is neither before, during, nor after. *The Man Who Fell to Earth* presents the complete movie time machine in action."

If this were not enough, Mayersberg continues:

> *The Man Who Fell to Earth* is an extravagant entertainment. It has dozens of scenes that go together, not just in terms of plot, but also like circus acts following one another; the funny, the violent, the frightening, the sad, the horrific, the spectacular, the romantic, and so on. We have clowns and lions and trapeze artists and dancing elephants and performing seals and ladies fired from cannons. The circus aspect of the movie is also, and in a rather different way, a game with time. It is all a matter of convention. Nobody talks of the non sequiturs of a circus because the plot isn't clear. The reason is that everybody knows the form at a circus. *The Man Who Fell to Earth* is a movie where we hope to introduce another form, or an interesting variation of an existing one, into the cinema. I don't know if there is a true antecedent of this film.[2]

And at times, Roeg seems actually to be pulling it off, managing to work in science fiction, sex, cowboys and Indians, government spies, film noir detectives, violence, political intrigue, romance, mystery, music, comedy, Elvis Presley, Terence Stamp, Gary Cooper, copulating lions, and carnivorous lizards. Unfortunately for most, however, Roeg puts so much into *The Man Who Fell to Earth* that he is ultimately unable to tie all the elements of the film together; because it never develops a strongly flowing narrative, traditionally developed characters or themes, or, most importantly, its own visual consistency, many people have a difficult time with the movie. In fact, Walter Rugoff, the film's American distributor felt that the movie was so confusing (especially after he cut twenty minutes for the American version) that he wanted to hand out mimeographed explanations of key scenes to audiences of the film.[3]

Despite Rugoff's problems with it, *The Man Who Fell to Earth* has a relatively straightforward plot. Because his own planet is in the throes of a horrible drought, Thomas Newton comes to Earth in the hopes of either bringing water back to his planet or investigating the possibility of migration. To finance his return trip home, he uses his advanced native technology to revolutionize our photographic and media equipment; in the process, he makes hundreds of millions of dollars and becomes, in the best Howard Hughes fashion, very secretive. In addition to arousing the public's curiosity, Newton and his company also begin to interest the government, who are afraid that Newton's unheard of ideas and products are flooding and upsetting the rest of the economy. So, as he is about to return to his planet, government agents kill his lawyer, Oliver Farnsworth, and imprison Newton. In their effort to make Newton explain who he is, the government enlists the help of his confidant and key scientist, Professor Nathan Bryce, and Newton's ex-mistress, Mary Lou. When Newton, who decides he has been mistreated and thus cannot morally cooperate with the investigators, refuses to answer questions concerning his identity, he is given a series of tests, one of which partially blinds him. Shortly thereafter, and for an unspecified reason, the government loses interest in his case; Newton wakes up to find the scientists and guards gone and wanders into the sunlight. Later, after the passage of an indeterminate amount of time, Newton, who is very drunk, and Bryce meet. Bryce asks him if he is bitter about the way people on Earth have treated him. "Bitter?" Newton answers, "No. We'd probably treat you the same if you'd come over to our place."

As this abbreviated summary shows, the plot, which may be unusual, should not present that much of a problem to the audience. And indeed, what seems to bother people is not the plot, but the way that Roeg chooses to tell his story. Rather than moving smoothly from one event to the next, Roeg almost hides the narrative flow among a series of tangential visual asides that allow him to incorporate all the various elements of his kaleidoscopic design. As Roeg himself describes it, "I think that one's life isn't like a Galsworthy story or a Priestly play, that flows on and on like this, a,b,c, and then she marries him and so on. It happens in little jagged moments; you walk up the street and break a leg and bump into a guy that tells you—and then you stay with him for five years and then you turn the corner and it goes past in jagged moments . . . this is a story about those accidents."[4]

So, instead of having time unravel gradually as we are used to, Roeg wants it to move "in fits and starts."[5] In other words, Roeg does not want to prepare us for an event by establishing its preceding causes and then by showing us its immediate consequences. Instead, he just shows us the event and lets us figure out for ourselves why it happened and what it meant. He does not, for example, have us follow the gradual deterioration of Mary Lou and Newton's relationship; although we know that they have problems, we are surprised by their violent quarrel and must supply for ourselves the reasons behind their resulting split. Because we are thrust into the event, rather than led into it, we are forced to adjust suddenly to what is happening on screen. One result of this is our inability to find a smooth rhythm to the film; it too moves in fits and starts. This in turn tends to make us view the film not as a coherent whole, but as a series of almost independent moments.

Sometimes, as in Newton's arrival on Earth, these moments can be absolutely brilliant. We hear no words, only Stomo Yamashta's eerie electronic sounds accompanying the low angle fish eye lens shot of Newton's feet tentatively making their way down a hill. As he makes his way down, the constantly moving camera picks up and pans towards a mysterious man, standing unnoticed on the top of another hill and monitoring Newton's progress. Next, Newton rests by a bridge and makes his way to the highway; as he turns to cross the road, he is almost knocked down by a car. From his reaction, we know he is scared and unfamiliar with the car; wherever he is from, it is not Earth. As he makes his way into Haneyville, he is accosted by a drunk and fixates on a huge, free-floating, and grinning inflatable face, no doubt an advertising gimmick for a now defunct business venture. Finally, Newton finds what he has been looking for, a store that will buy jewelry. Exhausted, he collapses lengthwise on the bench in front of the store and waits for it to open. Without one word of dialogue, Roeg is able to convey Newton's first moments on Earth. Through a careful selection of images and appropriately bizarre background sounds, Roeg creates an atmosphere that makes Earth look as strange and disorienting to us as it must to Newton.

Unfortunately, not all the sequences are this effective; although visually arresting, for example, Newton's meeting with Farnsworth serves no clear purpose. In the sequence, the film's third, Newton arrives at Farnsworth's home, presents him with some blueprints, and insists that Farnsworth, the country's leading patent lawyer, read them at once. While Farnsworth reads the blueprints and Newton watches, Roeg could tell us who Newton is and what his plans are. Instead, Roeg watches Newton plop two Alka-Seltzer-ish tablets into a glass of water, lingers on them as they fizz away, and, still without revealing any information, follows Newton as he walks to the window to see the sunrise. As Newton stares out into the city skyline, we are treated, for no apparent reason, to a montage of New York life, including a beautiful if trendy shot of the Chrysler Building, again popular thanks to the Art Deco revival. Although Roeg may be trying to stress the mass, anonymous nature of contemporary society that will eventually create a fear and distrust of Newton's individuality, the sequence seems more a leftover from *Walkabout* than anything else. As a result, Roeg may alienate and frustrate the viewer who, after twenty minutes or so, is ready for some information and some narrative consistency.

Our introduction to Bryce is even more striking and disconnected. Without any explanation of who he is, Bryce walks out of a university building, gets sneered at by a pretty young co-ed, and goes home. There he finds a birthday present from his daughter, a book on Impressionism. He opens the book to Breughel's painting of Icarus and Auden's "Musée des Beaux Arts," which describes how people see Icarus fall from the sky but, having places to go to, just turn and "sail calmly on."

Although the poem confirms that Newton comes from a distant planet and hints at Earth's indifferent treatment of him and at Bryce's ultimate refusal to help, the poem passes too quickly and comes too soon for us to do more than sense the connections it draws. For as soon as we have listened to the poem, which is read aloud by an unseen woman, but before we can begin thinking about it, Roeg has moved to a much more exciting and more visual sequence.

The professor puts the book away and begins to grade papers when, in the best thriller tradition, the door opens and someone quietly enters the apartment. Since Roeg switches to a subjective camera from the intruder's point of view, all we see are gloves, keys, and clothes dropping. As the figure gets closer to the professor, Roeg goes back to the objective camera; we see the same girl who sneered at Bryce drop a cloth over his head, pull him to the floor, and engage in a violent and rowdy bout of lovemaking, which she films with World Enterprise's (Newton's firm's) new self-developing film.

So far the sequence is fairly straightforward; we may not know who the professor is, but the connection between him and Newton is at least hinted at through the painting and poem. The connection is made explicit as soon as the girl and Bryce begin making love, though, because Roeg intercuts their sex with shots of Newton eating at an Oriental restaurant and watching a Kabuki duel between two swordsmen. The sequence's match cutting stresses the obvious similarity between the swords' and penis's thrusting. Soon both the duelists and lovers are done; as Bryce is about to climax, the swordsmen lose their balance and fall to the floor, also spent.

The scene offers, of course, several implications. Like the Orientals, who are only giving the illusion of a duel, Bryce is just going through the motions of love and passion. His lovemaking is violent, ungraceful, and fast; as soon as it is over, he routinely returns to grading his papers, suggesting that the lovemaking was superficial and only momentarily satisfying. Although we could have gotten the same impression by having the lovemaking scene stand on its own, ending as it does with Bryce grading the papers, the Oriental swordsmen add a visual texture to the film, as well as preparing us for Newton and Bryce's relationship.

Other sequences, however, do not fare so well. Not only are they thematically and narratively dispensable; they are visually static as well. One such scene is the one where the professor discovers Newton's identity. From the beginning, Bryce has suspected Newton's extra-terrestrial origins; when he asks Newton if he is from Lithuania, we sense that Bryce knows Newton's secret already. Since Bryce is a scientist, however, he is only satisfied by empirical evidence; to confirm his suspicions, he rigs an X-ray camera to his television set and gets Newton to sit in front of it. Unaware that Newton can see X-rays, Bryce tricks him into having his picture taken.

Although this scene does tell us that Newton is affected by X-rays and shows us how he communicates with his family through his appearances on television commercials, the scene takes too long to sustain our emotional reactions. We must watch the professor go through a tedious mechanical process to verify a fact that we already know and that he already suspects. Had the scene been shorter, we might have felt more protective of Newton, who is being violated, or have had a clearer response to the professor, who may or may not be justified. As it is structured, however, the scene has a flat, objective, and almost indifferent quality; rather than developing our response to either of the characters, it bores and loses us.

Even more damaging is the overlong and obviously derivative chronicling of Newton's imprisonment. Nothing, we see, has changed since *Performance;* the organization, which by now has become a nebulous conglomerate of big business and government, tries reason to get World Enterprises to play within their rules. After reason fails, the organization decides some further action is "appropriate." "Well," the boss says, "we're flexible. Something elastic. But remember, we're not the Mafia. This isn't some archaic Italian joke. We're determining the social ecology. This is modern America; we're going to keep it that way." But the result of such lofty rhetoric is, as we should have expected, the brutal murder of Farnsworth and his bodyguard/companion, Trevor, and the incarceration of Newton on the eve of his spaceflight.

The scene of Newton being mobbed at the launching pad is one of the film's most exciting; Farnsworth, Trevor, and the barbells being thrown out of the high-rise apartment has all the power, humor, and cinematic beauty of the violent scenes of *A Clockwork Orange.* Especially after these brilliant moments, Newton and our imprisonment in the self-consciously weird rooms becomes suffocating. As with the professor's exposure of Newton, the step-by-step documentation of Newton's decision to take a moral stand seems plodding, contrived, and boring.

Possibly because the government is afraid of charges of a cover-up, they place Newton in the wing of an old hotel that has been reconverted into a bizarre prison-research center highly reminiscent of the final sets in *2001.* Newton, clad in a tennis outfit, wanders around from room to room, drinking and looking at a wall painted to resemble a forest, complete with leaves on the floor; lies listlessly in bed watching television; or is strapped to a table while a team of doctors examine and question him.

Bryce, who watches the doctors torture Newton, refuses to help him. Instead, he finds Mary Lou and tries to convince her to see Newton and convince him to talk. When Mary Lou goes, however, her arguments and offers of a deal only convince Newton that he has already "proved enough." "I've proved everything I'm gonna prove. I've gone as far as I'm going." Then, in an emotional exchange, the two tell each other that they no longer love each other. As if to say

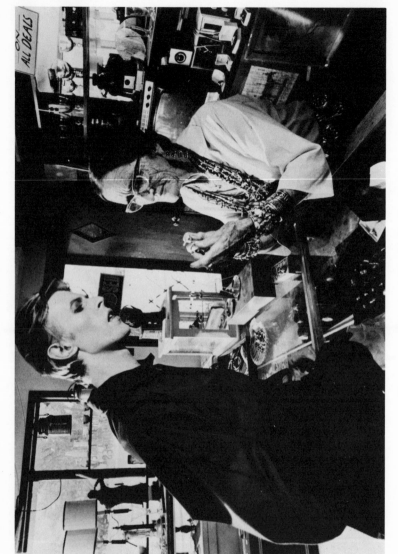

Newton pawns his ring and makes his first buck.

good-bye, Newton gives Mary Lou what we assume to be his last ring, "the only thing that's really mine to give." It does not, however, fit Mary Lou's hand; she throws it away and runs from the room.

Because this sequence represents Mary Lou's betrayal of Newton, the final step that forces Newton into his existential refusal to cooperate, and the final defection that leaves Newton totally alone, the scene should be a very effective one. Because, however, we have been cooped up like Newton in his claustrophobic prison and have already adjusted to Roeg's random and quick style preceding this scene, we lose patience with his inconsistent meticulousness and gradual unfolding of this sequence. And although we can feel with Newton the drudgery of his incarceration, we become too tired of it to be really moved or convinced by Newton's refusal to cooperate.

Also misstructured and thus wasted in the sequence are Roeg's handling of the witness and of the scientists' final action against Newton. The scientists seem interested in some confirmation that Newton actually fell to Earth by himself. As Newton repeats that he came alone and unseen, we remember the mysterious witness from the film's first scene; in case we forgot, Roeg cuts back to the shot of the man watching. If properly handled, the witness could have assumed some sort of cosmic irony; it has enough potential even to serve as the film's climax. Rather than develop the detail to its full effect, however, Roeg sandwiches the witness in between so many other events that it becomes just one more detail to get through.

Newton's contact lenses becoming stuck (because of the X-rays) works, or does not work, in the same way. It is the final mistreatment of Newton by the scientists and will force him to remain on Earth forever and also to lose his sight. We see how afraid Newton is of the X-rays; he is willing to tell them everything if they relent. When they agree to let him take out his lenses, his hands shake too badly to handle the tweezers. But when the X-rays are administered, rather than scream that he has been blinded, Roeg instead has him tell us that his lenses are now stuck, that he cannot ever get them off. Rather than be horrified by the scientists' actions, we have to stop to think about what having his lenses stuck means. By making the action a little too obscure, Roeg throws us out of an emotional reaction and into an intellectual one—at a time when he is sorely in need of our emotional response.

Thus, in the incarceration sequence, we should have reacted strongly at least three times. When Newton refuses to answer any more questions, he is taking a painful, existential moral stand. He has been manipulated, betrayed, and abused and has decided, within his limited means, to resist. But because the movie has become so cluttered by this time, we are too exhausted and confused to recognize the importance or drama of Newton's decision. Similarly, when Newton is asked to produce a witness that would substantiate his claim that he fell to Earth by himself, the fact that he does not even know of the witness is lost because it is simply thrown at us; rather than isolate or linger over it so that we could savor its irony, Roeg just presents it and moves on. And finally, when Newton is partially blinded, we should be feeling his pain more than at any other point in the film. Rather than having him cry out that he cannot see and thus reinforce the horror of the scientists' actions, Roeg mutes our response by having Newton's contact lenses stick to his eyes. Because we are uncertain as to what this means, we are unnecessarily removed from Newton's situation.

What is happening to us in this scene, then, is that, instead of having our reactions focused on Newton, we are being thrown this way and that. Rather than developing a sustained identification with Newton, the mass of details and compressed, almost objective reporting of the incarceration do not give us time to react. Rather than select and direct our attention to the most important and dramatic elements of this part of the movie, Roeg wastes too much time, sometimes showing us too much, sometimes too little. As a result, the sequence's dramatic potential is never realized.

As misstructured as this scene is, even its shortcomings seem inconsequential when compared to the scenes of Newton's dreams of his own planet and family. With the exception of these scenes, one of the film's strongest and most surprising qualities is its ability to present convincingly and assertively a story about an alien who learns about Earth through television and comes here in search of water. Eschewing the gadgetry and hocus-pocus of most sci-fi movies, *The Man Who Fell to Earth*'s modernistic but recognizable sets and matter of fact treatment of Newton, who is not so different from a Earthling, make this story believable even to those of us not normally sympathetic to the genre's subject matter.

When Roeg particularizes Newton's planet, though, he risks losing this part of his audience, at least for the duration of these scenes.

As long as we do not have to confront in concrete visual terms the concept of an alien falling to Earth, we can accept Newton; when we actually have to see his planet, the task becomes much harder.

To make matters worse, Roeg's presentation of Newton's planet and family is marred by an excessive sentimentality and occasional absurdity that gives us little reason even to want to believe in the scenes. When Newton drives in the country, for instance, he looks at a field and sees a horse running in slow motion. Suddenly, the soundtrack, which has been playing authentic, gritty music, shifts to the Brothers Four's "Try to Remember," a syrupy "make out" song from the mid-Sixties. While we listen to the song, we see Newton remember how his family used to play in the fields of his home. Done in the style of an Impressionist painting (remember Breughel), the scene is unavoidably trite and unsuccessful, evoking groans and derisive laughter from the audience. At least while the scene is on the screen, Roeg has lost us.

Some of the other images work the same way. Newton's spaceship does not bear the familiar yet exciting beauty of those in *Star Wars* or of the other flying saucer movies. Instead, it looks more like a goat-skin tent thrown over a clothesline. While Roeg's desire for a new look in interplanetary travel excites admiration, his vehicle does not. Again, as we look at this unbelievable and ineffective representation of Newton's world, Roeg loses us.

Far more critical is the intrusion of the alien's love-making habits in the final sex scene (of the American version). In it, Newton, who has decided to show Mary Lou what he really looks like, takes off his fake nipples and nails, removes his wig and his contact lenses, and faces her in full alien appearance. Mary Lou is understandably shocked; she screams and huddles in the corner. After a minute, however, she makes a tentative effort at touching him and even at making love. This effort on her part is moving and courageous; her ultimate inability to sustain any physical contact with him should be one of the film's most powerful, most intense moments.

Its emotional impact is diluted, however, by Roeg's intercutting to Newton's remembrance of how he and his wife make love, a process that can best be described as the mutual splashing of mud on each other's bodies. Again Roeg makes his image too concrete to be believable; he stretches our credibility by interjecting an un-necessary, obtrusive, and somewhat ridiculous visual reality on a concept better left to our imaginations. Had he left the alien's lovemaking out and concentrated on Mary Lou's reaction, had he made the alien's lovemaking habits less specific and alien, or had he for once shot a sex scene without intercutting to something else, Mary Lou's terror and physical incompatibility with Newton would have been devastating. Now, however, the scene seems too contrived to be very effective.

Roeg may not even need to eliminate all the visual references to Newton's planet; a quick, almost subliminal shot of his wife and children sprawled out on the ground could be retained, as could Newton's alien appearance. Roeg does, however, need to be much more selective with the shots. As they stand, they stretch the film's credibility and detract from much of its power.

One of the hazards of using an episodic structure, though, is that some episodes will inevitably be weaker and less effective than others. Many times, this can be compensated for by using each episode to build on the whole.

This refusal to tie himself to a larger structure results in characters that are thoroughly dispensable to the movie as a whole. Peters, the black man who engineers World Enterprises's downfall, is one of these characters. Although he is in the film for only several minutes, a good portion of that is a gratuitous shot of him diving nude into his swimming pool and into an embrace with his white wife and an equally gratuitous shot of him wondering if "we do or say the right things." Since he is just a henchman, we have little reason to care about him or to endure his moral twinges. Rather than missing him, we are glad that he goes away, undeveloped, almost as soon as he appears.

Although much more important to the story than Peters, Bryce is also surprisingly incapable of moving or interesting us. Through him and his probing of Newton's origins and knowledge, we learn almost everything we know about Newton, about how he can see where previous aliens have landed and walked (which explains the time warps that let Newton and the pioneers from the past see each other), why he came to Earth in the first place, and how, through television, he and his family were able to learn about Earth and, they hope, to remain in communication while Newton is on Earth.

Because Bryce has access to that information, he enjoys a privileged relationship with Newton. By the end of the film, however, he sells Newton out, even to the point of enlisting Mary Lou in the effort to get Newton to talk. As we watch him trick Newton into having his picture taken with the X-ray camera and see him walk away from the screaming, bound Newton, we should hate Bryce more than any other character in the film because, more than any other, he represents us Earthlings at our weakest, most callous, and most disgusting.

Regardless of his complicity in Newton's destruction, though, Bryce is incapable of provoking an intense emotional reaction from us. For all his ranting about the imagination, for all his contempt for less curious, more accepting, and less thinking people, he remains, as he describes himself, "a walking cliché, the disillusioned scientist," incapable of any emotion beyond a skeptical curiosity. So, because we realize that in the end he is just being true to his species and his kind, because Newton forgives him, and because the entire movie is too unfocused to get us that personally involved, Bryce fails to move us and thus escapes our justifiable hatred of him.

Although less important to the film, Farnsworth is a far more interesting and memorable character. A successful, near blind lawyer with a passion for music, he is a refreshing cynic, constantly aware and open about his desire for money and its accompanying power. He does not care about Newton's origins, but about Newton's intentions and how much they will affect Farnsworth's own financial status.

Farnsworth may care most about money but in his own way "feels sorry for," likes, and remains loyal to Newton. In an effort to make Newton's life more pleasant, Farnsworth never stops trying to turn Newton into a music lover (giving Roeg several chances to tease us into wondering whether or not Bowie will sing; he never does). In addition, we must respect Farnsworth for his resistance of the government's demands that he corral World Enterprises; even though he is motivated as much by his own financial interest as by his loyalty to Newton, Farnsworth still exhibits an admirable, if fatal, individuality.

More than to any action of his, however, we respond to Farnsworth's striking visual image. Although Bryce looks like any other aging, pot-bellied man, Farnsworth wears outrageously thick glasses that enlarge and highlight his eyeballs and can spit bubbles of saliva from his tongue. And in addition to enjoying a peculiar, verbally undefined, but visually suggestive relationship with Trevor, his bodyguard/companion, Farnsworth dies in a magnificent, unforgetable fall. Because of these unique physical and visual qualities, we find him much more unusual, cinematic, and intriguing than stodgy old Professor Bryce.

Despite his appeal, however, Farnsworth remains a minor character, incapable of doing much more than entertaining us while on screen. Mary Lou, on the other hand, as one of the film's two major characters, plays a far more important role in the film's ultimate impact on us.

Mary Lou is many things: comical, dumb, decent, vulnerable, sad, aware, drunk, loving. When we first meet her, she is responding to what she thinks is Newton's heart attack—by jamming the elevator and then carrying Newton down the hall to his hotel room. The shot is especially strange; as she cradles him and staggers down the hall, we think simultaneously of Christ symbolism, maternal behavior, and silent film comedy. We cannot figure out how Roeg wants us to respond; even though we realize the seriousness of the situation, the sight of her carrying Newton in her arms makes us laugh, even though we are not sure that is what Roeg wants us to do. But when Newton vomits in front of the camera, we stop laughing and, in a more sober mood, begin to notice Mary Lou's genuine concern for the stranger's welfare. Before long, her cheerfulness and her instinctive humanity have won us over.

By the time that she hints to Newton that she wants to spend the night with him, she has already revealed her weakness for gin. We can tell that she has been the victim of too many one night stands and too much rejection. She does not, however, sink into self-pity; the dismal quality of her relationships does not make her pathetic, only vulnerable. After Newton refuses to respond to her hints and gently asks her to leave, Mary Lou asks him what his name is; she has forgotten. "Sussex," Newton says, hiding behind his alias. "I don't know why, but I just can't remember that name." It is as if she knows that is not his true name; that she is capable of arousing such a suspicion suggests that she has more complexity and native intelligence than her appearance, speech, and demeanor initially indicate.

As she leaves, Roeg follows her out into the street and eavesdrops on her. "They always seem to lead such interesting lives, people who travel," Mary Lou says to herself. "People who write stories must lead kind of interesting lives too. I know I'll never be like a character in a story. I'll just be like everyone else. But maybe, maybe, why, I don't know. Maybe someday."

This scene works on two levels. Mary Lou is, of course, a character in a work of art dreaming about being a character in a work of art. As such, there is a certain innate irony to her remarks. But more important, although she is an aging, lonely, and poor woman with a drinking problem, her wistful yearning confirms her hidden intelligence and gives her an air of persevering innocence and wasted potential that becomes truly moving.

This quality is enhanced by her love for Newton, who likes but never really loves her. In the beginning, she is willing to have him on any terms and does not care that he does not return her love. But as time goes by, Mary Lou finds herself increasingly less satisfied with the material possessions Newton gives her; she needs instead his love. And when that is not forthcoming, more and more gin.

Since Newton is a family man genuinely in love with his wife, he is unable to love and thus satisfy Mary Lou. As the relationship deteriorates, Mary Lou resorts to outlandish hairstyles and a constant flow of drinks. She does not, however, have enough strength to give him up; so she refuses to leave or to let him go, even if it means she must hit him and rip his clothes, make disparaging remarks about his wife's sexuality, and humiliate herself. Newton, who cannot return her love and cannot cope with her inability to accept the relationship on his terms, finally does leave her, but only after he makes sure she will be financially secure for the rest of her life. When Farnsworth tells her of the generous arrangements, however, Mary Lou cries and says that she does not care about the money and only wants Newton—the one thing he cannot offer.

Because Mary Lou is such a decent character caught in such a familiar, emotional, and tragic situation, we care about her. But even her effectiveness is not as powerful as it could be. Instead, from the first moments we meet Mary Lou, Roeg has been carefully distancing us from her; by the end of the film, we may feel sorry for her, but we have also separated her fate from ours.

From the beginning, Mary Lou has a tackiness about her that, however endearing, prohibits us from identifying too closely with her. While Newton is allowed to be sophisticated and reserved, Mary Lou is just a little too vulnerable, too loud, and too revealing. Because she is destined to be disappointed and because her wants are so modest and simple, any association with her will bring us pain; in an almost defensive action, we instinctively distance ourselves from her. As a protective measure, we and Roeg assume an undeservedly superior and condescending attitude towards Mary Lou.

This can best be seen in the church scene. Mary Lou begs Newton to go to church not because it is the proper thing to do, but because she really believes in it. "It makes me feel so good," she says. "It gives me something to believe in. Everybody needs to add a meaning to life. I mean, when you look at the sky at night, don't you feel that somewhere out there, there's got to be a God. [Camera slowly moves in on her.] There's just got to be."

Although a potentially simple and moving statement of faith, Roeg undercuts the sincerity behind her words by having her look at the glass of gin as she talks about adding meaning to life. Then, when she looks at the stars and talks about God, she sighs and clouds her declaration in a stereotypical school-girl awe of the cosmos. And in the background the final strings from "Fascination" are playing, the musical ending to the campy Fifties' love story on the television.

These embellishments, from the gin to the television to Mary Lou's starry-eyed expression, make Mary Lou seem old-fashioned, romantic, and a little corny. When, on the other hand, Newton speaks about his beliefs, Roeg eliminates all such touches of melodrama and satire; when Newton tells Bryce that "I'm not a scientist but I know that all things begin and end in Eternity," a pronouncement not so terribly different from Mary Lou's, the camera does not catch his dreamy expressions or pan to a romantic shot of the universe. Beacause Newton is suave and knowing enough to couch the doctrine in acceptable rhetoric and in a flat yet assertive tone, Roeg and we in the audience have much less trouble accepting his faith. Because Mary Lou still sees the universe in unhip, traditional pictures of God, not eternity, and because her rationale for believing is so open, basic, unadorned, and unsophisticated, we would almost be embarrassed by her simple faith. So that we do not have to confront it, Roeg shields everyone; his details let us laugh gently at her while keeping her quaint and cute. And although he in fact may be protecting her and keeping her more appealing, his refusal to let Mary Lou state her beliefs with the same simplicity and objectivity that Newton gets is a patronizing gesture of Roeg's that creates a distance between Mary Lou and us.

There are less subtle reasons why in the end we divorce ourselves from Mary Lou. Like Bryce, she sells Newton out, agreeing to go to him and use her influence to get him to co-operate with the government. She tries everything, regardless of the pain she is causing him (in the American version). "Tell me one thing that you have on your planet that we don't have on ours; c'mon. You don't have any money; you don't have any water; you don't have any grass; you don't have any booze. What do you want to go back to a desert for? If you want desert, we got deserts here. This country's rich; we've got everything. . . . All right, I know. Your wife and your family. But by the time you get back, they'll probably be dead."

After this does not work, she tells him that Bryce will make a deal; all Newton has to do is prove who he is and then "I'll bet you you could probably go back. They'll probably let you go back. I'm sure they would. You could get on that little rocket ship of yours and go back. Huh?"

Finally, when this does not work either, Mary Lou goes to him and unbuttons his shirt; when all else fails, rely on sex. But when Newton moves away from her and rejects her advances, Mary Lou bitterly tells him that "I don't love you anymore." Although Newton calmly tells her that he too does not love her, our attention is focused on Mary Lou. She has betrayed Newton and, in the process, humiliated herself.

She has also lied. When Bryce talks Mary Lou into going to see Newton, the television in the background is playing the betrayal scene from *The Third Man*. As Mary Lou says, "I don't want to hurt him anymore. Poor Tommy's been hurt enough," her true feelings are being revealed in the older film's dialogue. "I don't want him anymore. I don't want to see him, hear him. But he's still part of me, that's a fact." No, regardless of what she says, she still cares about him. And because she does, because she has gone through so much to end up with so little, we cannot hate her. Like Newton, all we really can do is feel sorry for her.

What separates us most from Mary Lou, however, is not her action or fate, but the way Roeg has her age. So that Roeg could develop his new concept of time, he planned for his characters to age at varying rates, keeping only Newton and the sets chronologically constant. He almost succeeds; Farnsworth, Trevor, Bryce, and Peters age at random, almost unobtrusive, and convincing rates. Mary Lou, however, ages at a more accelerated and thus more noticeable speed; by the end, and partially thanks to a particularly poor make-up job, she has become such a caricature that we cannot

take her seriously. Because she looks so absurdly, unnaturally hag-
gard in the incarceration scene and with Bryce, we cannot really
believe in her. And because we cannot believe in her, we also lose
the ability to feel for her. So in the end, her power to move us is
sabotaged not just by her role and Roeg's style, but also because of
Roeg's concept of variable time.

Ultimately, then, the film must rest upon our reaction to Tommy
Newton, the man who falls to Earth. His attempts to get back to his
planet and his efforts to cope with the Earthlings' treatment of him
comprise the main plot and theme of the movie. In addition, Newton must carry the bulk of Roeg's peripheral statements about the
media and the world and receives the camera's attention more than
any other visual image in the film. But, as we shall see, for all that,
he too is kept at a distance from us; he too remains relatively remote
and unaffecting.

Despite his being from another planet, Newton should be an easy
character to identify with. To minimize his extraterrestrial origins
and maximize his somewhat ordinary personality, Roeg reminds us
that Newton is not much different from us. When Newton offers, for
example, to replace Farnsworth's antiquated stereo equipment with
some of his—at cost, of course—Farnsworth remarks that "maybe
he's not so different from us, after all." When Mary Lou asks what
his children are like, Newton replies, "They're like children.
Exactly like children." Unlike the aborigine in *Walkabout* who
never explains his actions, Newton tells us everything. We know,
for instance, why he comes to Earth and why he wants to go back
home; we know why he cannot go home and why he refuses to
cooperate; we even know how he makes love. In fact, Newton's
efforts at adjusting to his new culture, his longings for his estranged
family and concern for their welfare, and his refusal to mistreat and
hate any of us Earthlings all make Newton a likeable person with
whom we should be able to empathize and be moved by.

Although the potential for an identification with Newton is there,
however, we are not able to identify strongly with him; we are rarely
moved by his plight and feel only a detached interest and concern
for him. And, as in our reactions to *Performance* and *Walkabout*, our
relative distance is not a result of our boredom, but of Roeg's design.

At the end of *The Man Who Fell to Earth*, Bryce asks the drunk
Newton if he feels bitter about "everything." "Bitter?" Newton says,
"no—we'd have probably treated you the same if you'd have come

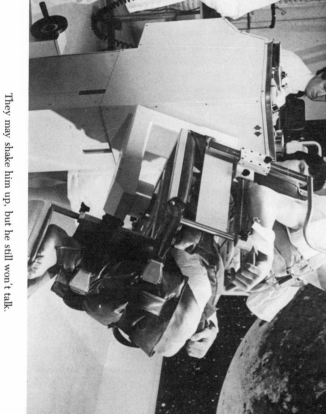

They may shake him up, but he still won't talk.

over to our place." So, although Newton has not given up hope that he will someday return to his planet ("Of course there's a chance, Mr. Bryce. You're the scientist; you must know there's always a chance"), he is resigned to the probability that he will remain on Earth forever. Still, he bears no malice for the people who are responsible for that fate.

Since Newton is not angry, but is tolerant and accepting of his situation, we too should feel that same benevolence. Had we too closely allied our fates with Newton's, the temptation would be the opposite, to hate Bryce, Mary Lou, and all the other paranoid humans who falsely feared and mistreated Newton. Thus, Roeg needs to tell the story in such a way that we understand what happens to Newton but do not take it personally or identify too strongly with him.

Roeg's method of telling a story in fits and starts, focusing on and isolating the events themselves instead of their causes and effects, helps make sustained identification with Newton impossible. In a movie like *Rocky*, for instance, where identification with the hero is critical, audiences spend a great deal of time seeing how Rocky is both a prisoner and tribute to his environment, how he is cheerful, sensitive, and kind to ugly dogs, an unnoticed woman, and to the little people on the street. We are manipulated into liking him; by the end of the movie, because he has been presented as such a worthy and winning person, we cheer for him; his struggle has become ours. And if it has not, the movie seems shallow, naive, sentimental.

We do not get such manipulation in *The Man Who Fell to Earth*. Although Newton may be just as deserving as Rocky, he does not make funny jokes or warm his way into our hearts. Instead, Roeg keeps Newton a cold character, making sure we stay on the outside of his character, getting little reason for making Newton's story our own.

The chocolate chip cookie scene illustrates the detatchment that Roeg encourages. Newton tells Mary Lou that he must leave her or die. Mary Lou becomes almost hysterical, telling him that he is an alien, that refuses to understand how we in America live, that she will never let him go, and that his wife is "no bloody good." As soon as she tells him that, she realizes that she has said too much and hits herself on the forehead. By this time, Newton is leaning against a wall, crying. She goes to comfort him but he turns away. As he does, she reaches for him and accidentally rips his shirt, leaving his shoulder exposed. They both stand there sobbing; suddenly, the oven timer goes off, reminding Mary Lou that the chocolate chip cookies she is baking are ready. She walks to the oven, takes the cookies out, and offers them to Tommy, who is still crying and still exposing his naked shoulder. Instead of taking one, he looks at her, screams, and, in slow motion, knocks the cookie sheet out of her hands. The cookies fly up into the air, twirling high into the sky until they come down and, no longer in slow motion, crash to the floor.

This confrontation with Mary Lou should have a tremendous impact; it is, after all, the definitive argument between two people we like. The scene comes, however, as a bigger surprise to us than it does to Mary Lou; we know that Newton does not love Mary Lou and know, too, that he has been especially homesick, but we do not know that she has become that pressing a problem. Since we have not been prepared for the fight, we can only guess that Newton cannot deal with the guilt of having a mistress because he is a family man and also that Newton cannot cope with his inability to love Mary Lou, who loves and needs him. Newton could simply have outgrown Mary Lou, acting like Gary Cooper in *Love in the Afternoon*, when Coop says, "The trouble is, people get too attached to each other. Things drag on. Scenes, tears, everything gets so maudlin. I think people should always behave as though they were between planes." And although Newton seems too committed to his wife to agree with Cooper, he is in between planes, so to speak, and is having trouble satisfying Mary Lou's demands for a deep relationship.

At any rate, any explanation of Newton's actions involves considerable speculation on our parts; unlike Rocky's telling us exactly what happened so that we know how to feel about the events, similar information is just not provided in *The Man Who Fell to Earth*. And as we wonder why what is happening is happening, we are removed from a total identification with either Newton or Mary Lou. Instead of feeling with them, we are too busy thinking about the reasons for the break-up. That could never happen in *Rocky;* it is so dependent upon our total identification with the character that we cannot be allowed to think about the events. They have, after all, been so carefully structured that any meditation destroys that intricate and airy fantasy we are watching.

Roeg's denial of information is not the only thing hampering our identification with Newton and/or Mary Lou. In addition, Roeg makes the scene so staged, so stylized, and so surreal that we can only view it with detached amazement. Newton and Mary Lou do not have an old-fashioned screaming match, as have all the great screen couples from Fred and Ginger to McCabe and Mrs. Miller or more recently Francie Evans and Jimmy Doyle (New York, New York). Instead, Mary Lou and Newton move through a series of unusual, static, and almost choreographed poses of hostility. When Mary Lou refuses to let Newton go, she rips his shirt. Rather than hitting her or tearing out of the room, Newton, the movie star, stands immobilized by one wall, his face and shoulder turned towards the camera. As he stares into it, he is frozen into a beautiful statue, an icon of pain and beauty. In other words, the camera's attention elevates him from an ordinary character into an object of beauty and style. Newton is not like, for instance, Rocky. Once we get past his style, we realize that Rocky is Everyman, a representation of all our failures, hopes, and aspirations. Because he strikes this chord in us, he becomes our friend and even our hero. Newton does not work this way; although we can recognize certain admirable, even similar qualities of ours in him, he is too unusual, beautiful, and controlled, even as he stands crying by the wall, to be like us. He is a star, different and compelling.

The comparison to Rocky is useful here too. Rocky's appeal stems from his humanity beneath the image of an uneducated, small-time loser who gets a chance "to go the distance." The task of the movie is to get us past his style, or lack of it, past the dumb image and to the realization that he deserves the break because he is the underdog in all of us. Newton, as the repeated shots of Bowie/Newton's profile remind us, is different; he is compelling not because we see ourselves in him, but because he is so charismatic, cool, detached, and stylish.

This concept of style explains the film's final scene. Set in a tropical Hollywood-type resort, Newton looks particularly sophisticated as he sits by the pool in his wide-brimmed hat and handsome coat, casually draped around his shoulders. He may not be bitter, but he is quite drunk. When he drops the drink he was holding, a waiter comes over to tell Bryce that he thinks "maybe Mr. Newton has had enough." Bryce agrees; Newton smiles, hiccups, tips his hat in time to the cool jazz now on the soundtrack, and puts his head down on the table. We can no longer see his face, only the top of his hat.

Roeg holds this shot, which becomes the background for the credits. A wonderfully cinematic moment, it provides an unexpected and understated contrast to the rest of the movie's flamboyance. At once a melodramatic, theatrical, and grand gesture, it gives Newton/Bowie the mixture of self-consciousness, irony, and flair that makes him a star, by definition different from the rest of us.

As such, Newton becomes different too from Turner and Chas, who distance us because they are strange; from the aborigine, whose culture prohibits our interaction; or from the girl in *Walkabout,* who fails in her bid for freedom. With Newton, the separation happens because of his style, his use of the pose that deliberately creates a barrier between the inner emotions of the person and his outward image. In the end, Newton is one of those people we can look at but not touch or be all that touched by.

As should by now be suspected, Roeg does not use his detached characters and episodic plot to develop lucidly one theme or visual image. Because he ends with Newton's refusal to hate, whether it be from a genetic or personality predisposition, the idea of Newton's tolerant attitude is important; still, it could hardly be called the driving force behind the movie. The imagination and the individual are also talked about, as are the concepts of interplanetary travel, Kirlian photography, and the pervasiveness of mob rule and alcohol. But, as befits Roeg's kaleidoscopic ambitions for this film, no one idea is given exclusive or even sustained attention.

While that allows Roeg to cover a lot of ground, it also encourages us to respond to the movie in the same way that Newton responds to the televisions in the movie. Although he gets all his information about Earth from it, he finds out after he gets to Earth that "the strange thing about television is that it doesn't tell you everything. It shows you everything about life on Earth but true mysteries remain. Perhaps it's in the nature of television, just waves in space."

It may be just waves in space, but television quickly becomes *The Man Who Fell to Earth*'s most trustworthy indicator of how the characters really feel or are acting. When Mary Lou convinces Newton to go to church, Gary Cooper is seducing Audrey Hepburn and telling her that he will not stay forever; when Mary Lou and Bryce sell Newton out, they do so during the betrayal scene of *The Third Man;* when Newton watches his wall of televisions, one monitor that gets special attention is the one tuned to *Billy Budd,* foreshadowing both Newton's fate and attitude.

But more important than the individual images is their cumulative encroachment on Newton's mind. At one point, he looks at the televisions lined up in front of him and runs his hand up and down the remote control so that the images become blurred and indistinguishable. "Get out of my mind!" he screams. "Leave me alone!" They have begun to overload his mind, making it impossible for him to function properly.

That is exactly what *The Man Who Fell to Earth* seems to do to its audiences. Roeg shows us a wide range of subjects without the benefits of a tightly structured narrative, warm characters, or disciplined thematic development. Instead, he bombards us with a series of visual images that force us to react humorously one moment, seriously the next. Eventually, it becomes just too much for us to absorb; the kaleidoscope blows our fuses.

TOP: Things are not always what they seem.
BOTTOM: Inside the space-ship. "Are you Lithuanian?"

6

Nicolas Roeg

PERFORMANCE, Walkabout, Don't Look Now, and *The Man Who Fell to Earth* should not be thought of as anything more than the first group of films Nicolas Roeg has directed. But no matter how many films Roeg ends up directing, the core of his basic philosophy will no doubt still be contained in these four films; they are, after all, the films in which he develops his thematic interests and visual style.

Although Roeg's reputation is usually based on his brillance as a cinematographer and an obtrusively visual director, there is a surprising thematic continuity to his films, as well. Indeed, when taken together, the four films become an extended comment on the effects of a dislocating experience that thrusts the character into a new environment. And typically, the experience will be not just traumatizing, but devastating, especially since it will be accompanied by some sort of powerful conspiracy that must be coped with by the individual, isolated character.

In *Performance,* for example, Chas, an old-fashioned gangster who has become an anachronism in the new world of corporate crime, is being hunted down by his fellow gangsters. His efforts to escape the mob lead him to Turner, a fading rock star who favors an exotic, degenerate life-style. As Chas interacts with Turner in Turner's environment, Chas experiments with and reevaluates his attitudes on drugs, sex, and self. Although interested in Turner's world, though, Chas is hardly sophisticated in its ways; under the influence of both a hallucinogen and Turner's erotic appeal, he loosens his guard and, as a result, loses his identity as an individual. Through his disorienting experience at Turner's, he is taken over or, as Turner would put it, he enters into a merger with Turner's image.

Walkabout's dislocation is much more naturalistic and easier to understand, although still quite traumatic. Unspecified pressures of

"Here's looking at you, kid."

modern life trigger a father's mental breakdown; he drives his two children into the Australian wilderness, tries to kill them, and, when he fails, kills himself and burns up his car instead. And even though he does not kill the children, he leaves them stranded in the desert. Because the children have been trained for a civilized, urban existence, they are totally ill-equipped for their confrontation with nature; despite a courageous effort on their part, the girl and boy are about to die when the aborigine, whose home is the desert, miraculously appears.

On their subsequent journey back to civilization, neither the girl nor the aborigine successfully deals with each other's culture or norms; because they cannot get beyond the barriers of each other's cultures and communicate and cope just as two individuals, the aborigine commits suicide while the girl undergoes a spiritual death, failing to take full advantage of her experience in the wilderness yet remaining imprisoned by its memory. Although she cannot return to the walkabout, her exposure to the wilderness's beauty and the realization of her rude treatment of the aborigine give her a devastating awareness of the artificiality and sterility of her life in the city. She has had too much experience in each culture to be truly happy in either one; thus, she must live and conform to an existence that cannot ever be really satisfying.

In *Don't Look Now*, the conflict becomes more abstract and much more terrifying. Without warning, John Baxter, who has built his life on rational precepts, is thrust into a conflict with the supernatural. To survive, he needs to act on the messages his dead daughter is sending him and on the premonitions and ominous warnings a psychic gives him. Rather than listen to the signs, however, John refuses to surrender his rational norms and to look at the dangerous situation he is in. Thus he renders himself unable to act properly, remaining as he does in Venice, falling prey to the powers of evil, and dying.

Oddly, Laura, who does not have John's second sight but is not afraid to confront the supernatural, proves much more adaptable. When she is told that her daugher is trying to contact her, she accepts the message and the peace it brings. By the end of the movie, she has lost her husband, a man she loves very much, but her experience in Venice seems to have given her the strength to adjust to his death and to go on living.

John's disorientation is much more terrifying than Chas's strange,

elusive transformation or the *Walkabout* girl's quietly tragic imprisonment in city life. As unknown and frightening as it is, the
Australian desert is at least a tangible, natural environment with
visible dimensions and straight-forward challenges. On the other
hand, Turner's house and world are too bizarre and self-conscious to
work their way into our everyday realities and thus function as a
direct threat to our physical well-beings. With John, however, Roeg
stops dealing with small time gangsters, perverse shamans, and
adolescents and concentrates instead on a likeable, productive,
somewhat ordinary adult. At once, Roeg's tapestry becomes more
familiar, more involving, and more upsetting, even as Roeg moves
the encounter into uncharted and primal territory.

For the first time in a Roeg movie, we are able to feel a total
emotional identification with the character; for the first time, his
battle becomes ours. By withholding information and refusing to
structure his narrative along a strongly logical and rational
framework, Roeg creates a malevolent, confusing, and horrifying
atmosphere. No longer do we watch a disoriented character; we now
feel the disorientation ourselves.

We not only identify with John, though; we also realize that he
dies because he does not look at the forces that are acting on him.
We realize as well that we too will have to fight the same battle with
death in an indifferent or even hostile universe. As we watch John, a
character we care a great deal about, go through the conflict, we see
how limited our own options are; we can choose like John not to look
or can choose like Laura to adjust to a survival of an enigmatic,
unknown nature. Either way, the process seems as frightening as it
is dangerous.

Roeg pushes the theme of disorientation even further in *The Man
Who Fell to Earth*. In it, an alien falls to Earth. Armed only with a
second-hand knowledge of our world gleaned from watching television, Newton must cope with our strange planet. And although he
becomes prominent and wealthy enough to achieve the technology
necessary to build a spaceship that will take him back home, his
loneliness leads him to alcoholism and his isolation raises enough
suspicion to make our government detain him on Earth. When he
refuses to answer the scientists' questions about his origins and
intentions, the scientists' tests leave him partially blinded and
stranded on Earth, forever separated from his wife, children, and
home.

Unlike the terror of *Don't Look Now*, however, Roeg closes *The Man Who Fell to Earth* on a note of irony and cool, detached acceptance. Although Newton's experience is even more dislocating than John's, involving not just the supernatural but the inter-planetary, and Newton's fate even more hideous, involving not a quick death, but a slow, imprisoned one, Newton does not scream. No, since his fate is just the price an outsider must pay and since we all are outsiders, we perhaps should learn from Newton. Sit down, have another drink, smile, and tip your hat to the ways of the world. Why fight something you cannot change?

One of those aspects that we apparently can do nothing about, at least in Roeg's universe, is our destiny to cope with life alone, as isolated individuals. By the end of each film, the characters have seen their relationships destroyed or deteriorated. Chas has been swallowed by Turner while Pherber hides in a closet and Lucy wanders around downstairs; the aborigine is dead and the girl, although married, finds meaning only in a wistful and romanticized reminiscence of her long gone walkabout; John, too, is dead while Laura walks alone into the church; even though Mary Lou and Bryce live together, they "don't see each other much," while Newton is going blind planets away from his family, who have probably been dead of thirst for years anyway. It is a bleak view of human relationships; if we want comforting pictures of people growing old and comfortable together, we will have to look elsewhere.

The individual does not just have to cope with the hostile environment by him or herself, but must contend with conspiracies of unseen and unknowable dimensions. In *Performance*, Harry Flowers' mob is an overt conspiracy, threatening honest or at least individualistic business owners and forcing them into the organization. More important, Turner's relationship with Flowers and his need to incorporate Chas's image into his own raise the more frightening possibility that Turner and Flowers have from the film's beginning been drawing Chas into a wider, more tangled web.

The rules of the socio-economic game have not changed by the time we get to *The Man Who Fell to Earth*. When the unnamed government official gives the order to harness World Enterprises, he repeats Harry Flowers' reasoning, that the individual in today's world must be forced to join the fold so that all may work together. Although not as prominent an element of the film as in *Performance*, the conspiracy, which now includes the government as well as the underworld, helps create the climate of anti-individuality and xenophobia that leads to Newton's detention on Earth.

In *Walkabout,* which deals with the relationship of a young girl and a young aborigine while in the wilderness, there does not seem much chance for a conspiracy. In the sense, however, that the two are programmed by their individual cultures and thus are forced to act in a predetermined, inadequate, and ultimately destructive manner, they too can be seen as victims of a much larger, more powerful force. When taken metaphorically, society becomes an almost conspiratorial agent preventing a spontaneous reaction between the two youths.

It is in *Don't Look Now* that the notion of conspiracy reaches its most frightening and most developed form. In it, Roeg aligns an entire universe against John Baxter. As the network of coincidences and accidents forms, John's friends and family are all drawn into the process of events that lead inevitably to his death. With the church's helplessness and the police inspector's suspected complicity, the conspiracy by now has become too immense and omnipotent to fight. When it wants you, it will get you.

One way to deal with the conspiracy is, as Newton has done, to accept it and then drink yourself into oblivion. Another way to escape the conspiracies, the isolation, and the confusion, at least for the moment, is through art, the exercise of the imagination in the hopes of creating something beautiful, profound, and permanent. In each of the films except *Don't Look Now,* which can allow no such digression, Roeg uses a poem, song, painting, or story to give his movie a focus.

In *Performance,* for example, Turner derives much of his mystique from his rock-star style and is connected to Flowers by a painting that hangs on Flowers' office wall. More important, Borges' short story "The Old Man on the Mountain" explains the identity transformation and Chas's role in it. In fact, Borges may be thought of as *Performance*'s mentor; when Turner is shot and we get to see the old man inside Turner's head, the image is a picture of the Argentine writer.

In *Walkabout,* the white boy tells a story that we think must explain the movie; since he does not even get to finish it, however, it fails to provide the hoped for answers. But in the last moments of the film, a narrator recites Housman's lines about the "happy roads we walked but cannot come again." When taken along with the film's framing device, the croupier's announcement that the last chance to place bets has come and gone, the girl's walkabout and resulting fate is placed in an irrefutable perspective of a lost opportunity. Without the poem, the focus would have been much less clear.

What little focus *The Man Who Fell to Earth* has is achieved through various art forms, notably poetry and television. Breughel's painting of Icarus is shown with the partial text and oral reading of Auden's "Musée des Beaux Arts"; through it, we realize that Newton falls to Earth, makes surprisingly little impact on it, and does not fly away again. And through television and old movies, we learn that Mary Lou and Bryce will betray Newton and (through the *Billy Budd* excerpt) that Newton will be martyred but will bear his captors and judges no malice.

Even in *Don't Look Now,* Roeg uses art, but for a different purpose. The film's power would be diminished if Roeg or it provided us with an alternative to its events. Accordingly, art is portrayed as futile, empty, or ineffective; we see beautiful but decaying religious statues, mosaics, and crosses. However grand they used to be, they are now devoid of any power or meaning. God—and man—can no longer pretend that these objects are important "priorities" in the fight for survival.

Because Roeg uses art to further his film's designs, he is unlike the French New Wave directors and newer directors like Paul Mazursky and Brian de Palma, who pepper their films with references to their favorite books, movies, and artists. Rather than using his films as excuses to pay homage to his heroes ("I hate homages," Roeg has said), Roeg prefers to integrate the works of art into his films.[1] Once in, they comment on, reinforce, or explain the film. If they did not, they would not be there in the first place.

More important than Roeg's themes, however, is the visual style he has developed, no doubt because he was such a creative cinematographer in the years before he turned to directing. Even *Performance* has a visual identity and assurance that usually comes much later in a director's career. At any rate, a look at *Performance* and the three other movies can lead us to Roeg's style, which includes obtrusive editing, a loose and episodic structure, frantic and often unexplained cross and match cutting, an almost total disregard for transitions that provide motivation or smooth narrative continuity, and, above all, breathtakingly beautiful composition and images.

Almost always, Roeg's non-naturalistic editing serves to heighten the realism and effectiveness of the on-screen event because it captures the way we tend to see things in crisis situation. When the father falls down in a discontinuous motion in *Walkabout* or when the water buffalo dies in slow motion there; when Christine drowns in *Don't Look Now*, or when the food spills over Laura; when the scaffold falls in squeeze motion in *Don't Look Now*, when Chas kills Joey in *Performance* or even when Mary Lou and Newton fight in *The Man Who Fell to Earth*, we are startled not because the events look so staged, but because Roeg shows us the events as they would look if they were happening to us. Although an independent observer or an objective camera would not be able to manipulate time so as to restructure its flow—Christine would simply drown, the father would fall directly to the ground, the food would quickly spill—Roeg can. And through this manipulation of time, he is able to give the events an almost overwhelming realism and power.

He also makes extensive use of cross-cutting that connects events and characters visually before he connects them narratively. The first twenty minutes or so of *Performance*, for example, introduce each of the characters separately; because Roeg cuts from one character to another, we visually sense and accept that they are related. We must wait until later, however, for the information that intellectually explains how Chas, Turner, Harry, the lawyer, the gangsters, the girl are related. In *Walkabout* we do not know that the beginning montage's comment on the rigidifying effects of civilization will reverberate throughout the film until after the film is over. Until then, it operates primarily on a visceral, visual level. And when Roeg intercuts Bryce's lovemaking with the Oriental swordsmen at Newton's restaurant, we sense that Bryce and Newton will soon be connected; we just have to wait until Roeg is ready to tell us how.

Probably the most famous cross and match cutting in Roeg's films is in the most famous of all his scenes, the love scene in *Don't Look Now*. There, by intercutting John and Laura's lovemaking with their subsequent getting dressed and preparing to go out to dinner, Roeg is able to emphasize poignantly both the fleeting, moving beauty of their love and their ultimate isolation as two individuals, as well as to shift the focus of the movie from Laura to John. It is the film's best example of nothing being what it seems; even the simple, beautiful act of love assumes pregnant, even ominous overtones.

The scene is so effective, in fact, that it tends to obscure the other love scenes in Roeg's movies, all of which are intercut with some other activity. In *Performance*, the effect is hardly noticeable because the movie is shot from so many different points of view. Because we are almost always being simultaneously informed of Chas, Turner, Pherber, Lucy, and Flower's perspectives, the movie can be thought of as one extended cross-cut sequence; as such, the lovemaking scenes do not single themselves out for any special attention. In *Walkabout*, the nude scene that shows the girl swimming naked and for the first time really enjoying bodily pleasure is intercut with the two boys playing in the fields and gathering dinner; she is swimming nude, Roeg seems to be telling us, only because the "men" are occupied somewhere else. The sublimated sex scene, where the girl plays in the trees but sees legs and crotches, is intercut with the aborigines' discovery of the father's car. And the love scene, the final reverie about life in the wilderness, is contrasted to the now grown-up girl's dealings with her husband, who is boring her with his tales of office politics. Thus, through Roeg's intercutting of the girl's sexual fantasies with the repressive or oppressive presence of civilization, he reminds us that she never experiences the unbridled freedom of sex, that it is always imprisoned by some societal influence.

In *The Man Who Fell to Earth*, Bryce's lovemaking is intercut with the swordsmen, while Mary Lou and Newton's is intercut the first time with abstract colors and with a close-up of them looking at us and the second time with Newton's fantasy of the way his kind makes love. In both of Newton and Mary Lou's love scenes, the intercutting reminds us of the gap that always exists between them; even while in bed here, Newton would rather be at home.

In each lovemaking scene in each movie, then, Roeg uses sex not just as something beautiful and cinematic in its own right, but also as a means to some discovery about how the characters really feel or about the situations those characters are about to encounter. And perhaps more than any other single trait, these intercut sex scenes serve as Roeg's own, unique visual signature to his movies.

Partially because of the cross-cutting, partially because the visual connections are often made before the intellectual ones, partially because of the brilliant but obtrusive cinematography (as opposed, for example, to the brilliant but unobtrusive cinematography of Altman's *The Long Good-bye* or *McCabe and Mrs. Miller*), Roeg's films seem more loosely structured than they really are. Often the larger patterns that tie the films together are not apparent while we are watching the films, but come later in retrospect. This seems according to plan; as Roeg himself says, "I hope that films exist longer than the first week; that they don't just come and go, and if you don't get it you don't; that they have various stages of life . . . . the idea should be to give constant enjoyment to the film and for someone a year or so later to say, 'Hey, you know . . . .!' "[2]

So, in *Performance*, for example, what seems like a curious preoccupation with the color red (Chas trying to duplicate his lover's red beauty mark, Turner painting the walls red, Chas dying his hair, the screen going awash with red) later reveals itself to be an extended preparation for the identity transfer; the ever-present mirrors that looked like a visual hang-up of Roeg's are used, we learn towards the film's end, as a means of ascertaining the existence of the demon. In *Walkabout*, what appears to be an isolated and self-consciously surreal episode with the weather station becomes, through the editing technique of freeze frames, an integrated component of Roeg's statement on civilization, as well as a method of imposing a cinematic consistency onto the film. Similarly, although apparent only in retrospect, the beginning montage's shots of the school girls bouncing up and down in their desks illustrate the girl's discipline, a discipline that helps her endure but limits her adaptability. Although this and other shots like it, then, may initially seem to have no purpose, they actually are subtly related elements that, when taken together, give the movies their visual consistencies and identities.

Even in *Don't Look Now*, which in many ways is Roeg's least demanding and complex film, incidents that seem unrelated or hopelessly coincidental ultimately draw themselves into the film's tight pattern. The slide bleeding red, the glass breaking, the bicycle tire being punctured, John, Jr.'s finger bleeding, Christine drowning, the restaurant window flying open, the omnipresent color red by the end are all arranged into an inescapable, consistent, and identifiable sequence of events. Although Roeg may appear to be collecting striking but loosely associated images and to be interested only in creating a Gothic atmosphere, he is actually exercising a masterful control over the film's design.

Perhaps because of the film's grandiose attempts to tie all genres and movements of film history together, Roeg fails to exert this type of control over *The Man Who Fell to Earth*. For the first time, Roeg does not draw the film's visuals into an integrated structure; as a result, the whole seems much less than the sum of its impressive but isolated individual scenes. The montages of the swordsmen, the city, the covered wagons, Newton's space fantasies, the television sets never coalesce into a whole; the proliferation of loose ends suggests a film that has slipped away from Roeg.

Using Roeg's first three films (and Fellini's, Antonioni's, and the flock of experimental and experiential film-makers' movies, all of which refuse adherence to the demand that movies be closed, rational structures) as training, however, we should now be able to suspend our demand for thematic, narrative, or even visual consistency and just enjoy the episodes as they happen. After all, in *Performance*, we watch several stories unfold independently, only gradually learning how Chas, Turner, Harry, the lawyer, and the chauffeur are related; in *Walkabout*, we never get an explicit explanation for the father's problems, which motivate the entire film, or for the borigine's suicide. And in *Don't Look Now*, we are forced to replace our orientation towards rationality and probability with the film's focus on a more primal, non-rational, and supernatural perspective. Finally, in *The Man Who Fell to Earth*, Roeg asks us to go one step further. Now that we have learned to do without an intellectually and rationally satisfying structure, we should also be able to forego a demand for visual consistency, which is just a more sophisticated, more cinematic insistence on a tight, ordered structure.

When, then, Roeg fails not just to fill us in on causes, effects, and the gradual unfolding of events or character motivation, but also fails to impose a recognizable visual consistency on the film as well, he is only pushing the refusal for an adherence to rationality to its logical end. I am not trying to apologize for Roeg here, nor am I trying to make his every shortcoming or action a virtue. However, almost everyone has criticized the movie for its failure to develop a consistency that directs and focuses our responses. And we do seem to need that direction in order to be involved.

For whatever reason we make it, however, the demand for a visual consistency in film, like the color red in *Don't Look Now,* for example, is really no more than a sophisticated demand for a rationality or structure that provides identifiable form, be it intellectual or visual, to the movie. So, when we criticize the film for being a grab-bag that fails to consolidate our emotions or minds, we are operating from a bias for rationality in art, a reactionary, even literary bias that many of us may have thought had been conquered.

When seen from this light, the problem with *The Man Who Fell to Earth* stems more from us and our training than from the film. In fact—and perhaps unwittingly—Roeg has given us his potentially most revolutionary and fully realized movie in *The Man Who Fell to Earth.* By not only forcing us to reject our demand for an intellectually rational (or structured) movie, but also by insisting that we no longer ask for a visual consistency, which is a rationality of a different degree, not a different kind, Roeg rejects the notion that a movie must finish every idea it introduces or that it needs to be coherent. All it has to do is be itself.

The Man Who Fell to Earth, then, seems to be pointing to more abstract movies than we are used to seeing. And although both Robert Altman and George Lucas feel that is the direction movies may take once they and we are freed from our theatrical, literary, and rational biases, this entire philosophy still runs counter to the traditions we have been schooled in.[3] Because we are not used to the freedom it makes possible, we may yearn for the security of other, more conventional movies. But yearn as we might, we also must respond to Roeg's demand that we use our imaginations not just in the movies of the future, but today, in his movies.

This demand that we use our imaginations explains both Roeg's style and his limited commercial appeal. When Bryce talks about his college students, he calls them mindless, unimaginative, and programmed to accept exactly what is being fed to them. So that we do not respond lazily like the students, Roeg refuses to create irrefutable stimuli upon which our responses can be mechanically ordered. So that we do not identify with and get swept along by a character, Roeg gives us (with the exception of John Baxter) bizarre, remote, unpleasant, or unsuccessful characters; because we do not envy them or their positions, we maintain some distance from them. By not telling a direct, fast-paced, and complete story, Roeg also forces us to think about what is happening on screen and makes us supply some of our own causes and effects for the events. And by keeping his patterns more visual than verbal (the reds in *Performance* and *Don't Look Now*, the sunsets and freeze frames in *Walkabout*), he makes us watch, rather than just listen. On every level, then, he encourages active interaction with the film, not passive acceptance of it.

Because we are not used to working when we go to the movies, many people resent, ignore, and reject Roeg's style. Even if sympathetic to Roeg's goals, however, we may be unprepared to face our response to the film.

Pauline Kael seems to have done just that when she saw *Don't Look Now*. "Nicolas Roeg," her review begins, "employs fast, almost subliminal imagery in the new English film, *Don't Look Now*, and his entire splintering style affects one subliminally. The unnerving cold ominousness that he imparts to the environment says that things are not what they seem, and one may come out of the theater still seeing shock cuts and feeling slightly disassociated. The environment may briefly be fractured; for me ten minutes or so passed before it assembled itself and lost that trace of hostile objectivity. I don't recall having had this sort of residue of visual displacement from a movie before, but it's reasonable if one has been looking at a splintered universe for almost two hours."[4]

Now, to have an unparalleled emotional reaction from a movie is something to get excited about; however, as the subtle diminutives in this paragraph ("one may come out," "may briefly") hint, Kael spends the rest of her review denigrating the movie and complaining that the style is too good for the content, or lack of content. If after seeing the film she could not function, even if for just minutes, the film moved her as no other movie has before, then the movie must be spectacularly effective. So effective, in fact, that it brings with it the often unwelcome opportunity to re-evaluate our most basic assumptions about movies, art, and even life.

And, just as John is reluctant to acknowledge his second sight, a power that can be a curse "as well as a gift," we too may be unwilling to deal with many of the challenges Roeg presents. Are we, like Chas, erotically attracted to Turner and his world; are we, like the girl, incapable of creating a free, meaningful life or have we too missed our chance; do we, like John, refuse to acknowledge the non-rational and supernatural; do we demand a structure and answers to our movies and close ourselves off when not given one?

All are significant questions; often the answers, when there are some, may be difficult, unpleasant, and surprising. So, instead of coping directly with them, we may find it easier to act as Kael did this time and reject the movie itself as inferior and unworthy of more serious consideration. But for all her intellectualizations, Roeg elicited an amazing response from her; even though she chose not to pursue it, he did his job and did it well.

Because he is so good at obtaining such intense responses, it is particularly fitting that he uses rock music, electronic sounds, and rock stars so extensively in his movies. Rock, after all, is even more effective than the movies in its ability to obliterate the intellectual and the rational in favor of a more spontaneous and physical response. And, as the careers of David Bowie and Mick Jagger prove, rock can elevate the style or image to almost mystical heights. It is a medium that seems especially well suited to Roeg's cinematic aspirations.

Like rock music, Roeg flirts with violence, stylized poses, and images that, when appraised by the sane, realistic, and analytical eye, can look most infantile and shallow. But while the music is playing, the sounds, performers, and audience immerse themselves so totally that the pose, the violence, and the art become much more real than the more mundane existences left outside the theater or arena. And, as Kael found out, during the concert and for hours (or minutes, in her case), that illusory world assumes a substantive reality much more tangible and alluring than the flat, unimaginative, and predictable existences possible in the straight world.

In this attempt to have us see new things or old things in a new way, Roeg is asking no more of us than did Méliès, Clair, Vigo, Buñuel, Godard, Fellini, Antonioni, Meeker, Anger, and a parade of others. Although Roeg does not have these directors' academic respectability, he is one of the first, most tasteful, and most talented English speaking artists interested in and capable of making feature length, expensive films that do not compromise his artistic beliefs. Because he can do this, because he has a thorough training in film history and technology, and, most of all, because he, unlike the others, has the bulk of his film-making ahead of him, Roeg has a real chance at making or at least bringing us closer to a really new kind of movie. And that makes Nicolas Roeg's future critically important to anyone who cares about movies—today's, yesterday's, and tomorrow's.

Notes and References

Chapter One

1. New York, 1976, p. 18.
2. Terry Curtis Fox, "Nashville Chats: An Interview with Robert Altman," *Chicago Reader*, July 4, 1975, p. 10.
3. Mel Gussow, "Roeg: The Man Behind *The Man Who Fell to Earth*," *New York Times*, August 22, 1976, II, 12.
4. "Identity: An Interview with Nicholas Roeg," *Films and Filming*, 18 (January, 1972), 19. Subsequent page references incorporated into the text are identified by the name "Gow."
5. Tom Milne and Penelope Huston, "Interview with Nicholas Roeg," *Sight and Sound*, 43 (Winter, 1973/74), 5. Subsequent page references incorporated into the text are identified by the name "Milne."
6. Bosley Crowther, "*Dr. Crippen*," *New York Times*, February 15, 1964, p. 14.
7. A. H. Weiler, "*Nothing But the Best*," *New York Times*, July 14, 1964, p. 28.
8. "*The Masque of the Red Death*," *Films and Filming*, 11 (August, 1964), 20.
9. "*The Masque of the Red Death*," *New York Times*, September 17, 1964, p. 52.
10. Bosley Crowther, "*Far from the Madding Crowd*," *New York Times*, October 19, 1967, p. 59.
11. Alexander Walker, *Hollywood U.K.* (New York, 1976), p. 421.
12. *Variety*, November 25, 1970, p. 12.
13. *Ibid.*, October 20, 1971, p. 11.
14. From the advertisement of *Don't Look Now* in *New York Times*, December 9, 1973, II, 9.
15. Pauline Kael, "The Current Cinema," *New Yorker*, 49 (December 24, 1973), 68.
16. *Variety*, April 10, 1974, p. 12.
17. "*Don't Look Now*," *New York Times*, December 23, 1973, II, 15.
18. *Variety*, October 27, 1976, p. 14.

144

19. Tom Milne, *"The Man Who Fell to Earth,"* *Sight and Sound,* 45 (Summer 1976), p. 145.

20. All the quotations and information in these paragraphs are taken from Gussow's *New York Times'* article on *The Man Who Fell to Earth,* August 22, 1976, II, 12.

Chapter Two

1. Alexander Walker, p. 420.

2. *Variety,* July 31, 1970, p. 14.

3. Tom Milne and Penelope Huston, "Interview with Nicolas Roeg," *Sight and Sound,* 43 (Winter, 1973/74), 8.

4. Alexander Walker, p. 421.

Chapter Three

1. Gordon Gow, "Identity: An Interview with Nicolas Roeg," *Films and Filming,* 18 (January, 1972), 21.

Chapter Four

1. Tom Milne and Penelope Huston, "Interview with Nicolas Roeg," *Sight and Sound,* 43 (Winter 73/74), 3.

2. Charlie Haas, "Learning to Love *The Texas Chain Saw Massacre,"* *New Times,* 10 (May 13, 1977), 64.

3. Charles Champlin, "A Roeg's Gallery of Imagistic Motion Pictures," *Los Angeles Times Sunday Calendar,* September 12, 1976, p. 29.

4. Haas, p. 66.

5. Milne and Huston, "Interview," 8.

Chapter Five

1. *Rolling Stone,* No. 246 (August 25, 1977), 25.

2. "The Story So Far . . . ," *Sight and Sound,* 44 (Autumn, 1975), 231.

3. Gussow, *New York Times,* p. 12.

4. John Lifflander and Stephan Shroyer, "Nick Roeg," *Andy Warhol's Interview,* 3 (March 1976), 35.

5. Mel Gussow, *New York Times,* August 22, 1976, II, 12.

Chapter Six

1. Tom Milne and Penelope Huston, "Interview with Nicolas Roeg," *Sight and Sound,* 43 (Winter 73/74), 8.

2. Milne and Huston, 8.

3. Terry Fox, "Nashville Chats," *Chicago Reader,* July 4, 1975, p. 10 and "The George Lucas Interview, *Rolling Stone,* No. 246 (August 25, 1977), 50.

4. Pauline Kael, "The Current Cinema," *New Yorker,* 49 (December 24, 1973), 68.

Selected Bibliography

AITKEN, WILL, "Icarus Drowned," *Take One*, October, 1976, pp. 38–39. A somewhat negative review of *The Man Who Fell to Earth*.

BARTHOLOMEW, DAVID, "The Man Who Fell to Earth," *Film Heritage*, 12 (Fall, 1976), 18–25.

CANBY, VINCENT, "*Don't Look Now*," *New York Times*, December 9, 1973, II, 56.

———, "The Man Who Fell to Earth," *New York Times*, August 22, 1976, II, 2.

———, "*Walkabout*: A Tribal Study in Survival," *New York Times*, July 2, 1971, I, 26. (Reviews.)

CHAMPLIN, CHARLES, "A Roeg's Gallery of Imagistic Motion Pictures," *Los Angeles Times Sunday Calendar*, September 12, 1976, pp. 1, 29. One of the first and still one of the only comprehensive newspaper articles to treat Roeg's career as a whole and to regard him as a major new force in films.

DEMPSEY, MICHAEL, "*Don't Look Now*," *Film Quarterly*, 27 (Spring, 1974), 39–43.

EDER, RICHARD, "The Man Who Fell to Earth," *New York Times*, May 29, 1976, V, 13.

FARBER, STEPHEN, "*Don't Look Now* Will Scare You Subtly," *New York Times*, December 23, 1973, II, 15. This rave review also provides the most concise, most insightful, and best assessment of Roeg's career to date. Anyone interested in Roeg and in excellent film criticism should read this article at least once.

———, "The Nightmare Journey," *Cinema*, 6 (Fall, 1970), 67–69.

GOW, GORDON, "Identity: An Interview with Nicolas Roeg," *Films and Filming*, 18 (January, 1972), 18–25. In each interview, Roeg has been articulate and revealing. Here, in addition to giving some interesting background on *Walkabout* and describing its aim to succeed both as a children's film and an adult one, there is the most informative description of Roeg's pre-directoral career we have. There is also a filmography of his work as a cinematographer.

GREENSPUN, ROGER, "Jagger and the Fox Shape," *New York Times*, August 4, 1970, I, 21.

GROSS, LARRY, "Film Apres Noir," *Film Comment*, July-August 1976, pp. 44–49. *Performance* as a modern film noir.

GUSSOW, MEL, "Roeg: The Man Behind *The Man Who Fell to Earth*," *New York Times*, August 22, 1976, II, 12. The definitive account of the cuts Rugoff made in the film, why he made them, and Roeg's reaction to the new version. Indispensable.

HAAS, CHARLIE, "Learning to Love *The Texas Chain Saw Massacre*," *New Times*, 10 (May 13, 1977), 60. Although Haas's article is about *Chain Saw*'s director, Tobe Hooper, Hooper's remarks seem directly applicable to *Don't Look Now* as well.

KAEL, PAULINE, "The Current Cinema," *New Yorker*, 49 (December 24, 1973), 68–70. The review of *Don't Look Now* discussed in this book is the final chapter.

KANON, JOSEPH, "Death in Venice," *Atlantic*, 233 (January, 1974), 94–96. (Review of *Don't Look Now*)

KINDER, MARSHA, and BEVERLE HUSTON, "The Ultimate Performance," in *Close-Up: A Critical Perspective on Film* (New York: 1972), pp. 359–376. Certainly the most valuable essay on *Performance*, especially helpful in its analysis of Borges' impact on the film.

KOLKER, ROBERT PHILLIP, "The Open Texts of Nicolas Roeg," *Sight and Sound*, 46 (Spring, 1977), 82–84. The most recent, most extensive magazine treatment of Roeg's career.

LIFFLANDER, JOHN and STEPHAN SHROYER, "Nick Roeg . . . and the man who fell to earth," *Andy Warhol's Interview*, 3 (March, 1976), 34–36. Although mostly about how Roeg feels about Jagger and Bowie, the interview also gets into Roeg's concept of film time, his idea that *The Man Who Fell to Earth* is a love story, and his respect for *Earthquake*'s technological and commercial virtuosity. In addition, it has the best photograph of Roeg I've seen.

McGREGOR, CRAIG, "*Walkabout*: Beautiful but Fake?" *New York Times*, July 18, 1971, II, 1.

MAYERSBERG, PAUL, "Story so far . . . *The Man Who Fell to Earth*: A Commentary by the Screenwriter," *Sight and Sound*, 44 (Autumn, 1975), 225–31. An invaluable guide to what he and Roeg thought the movie was going to encompass, this is also an interesting perspective on how the writer feels about his script when he realizes it is not the final product.

MILLAR, GAVIN, "*Walkabout*," *Sight and Sound*, 41 (Winter, 71/72), 48.

MILNE, TOM, and PENELOPE HUSTON, "Interview with Nicolas Roeg," *Sight and Sound*, 43 (Winter, 73/74). 2–8. This excellent article concentrates on *Don't Look Now*, but also touches on Roeg's feelings for Cammell, Borges, and homages. In addition, they get Roeg to talk about some of his projects that never got made.

MILNE, TOM, *"The Man Who Fell to Earth,"* *Sight and Sound,* 45 (Summer, 1976), 145–147. The most interesting analysis of *The Man Who Fell to Earth* that I have read, Milne tries to use the railroad as the key visual and thematic image of the movie. When, however, he applies "the end of the line" metaphor to the incarceration scene as a means to continue his argument, he seems to me to be forcing his point. Still, the article remains provocative to the end.

ROBINSON, DAVID, "Spellbound in Nicolas Roeg's Venice," *London Times,* October 12, 1973, p. 15.

SCHJEDAHL, PETER, *"Performance,"* *New York Times,* August 16, 1970, II, 1.

SIMON, JOHN, *"Performance,"* *New York Times,* August 23, 1970, II, 1. More than any other critic, Simon has been particularly unreceptive to everything about Roeg. Here is where the hate affair begins.

WALKER, ALEXANDER, "No Sympathy for the Devil," in *Hollywood U.K.: The British Film Industry in the Sixties* (New York: 1976), pp. 416–425. This is a fascinating account of the cast, crew, and business's reaction to *Performance.* Don't stop with this excerpt; the rest of the book is equally interesting.

Filmography

PERFORMANCE (A Goodtimes Production, Warner Brothers, 1970)
Producer: Sanford Lieberson
Associate Producer: David Cammell
Co-Director: Donald Cammell
Assistant Director: Richard Burge
Screenplay: Donald Cammell
Director of Photography: Nicholas Roeg
Music: Jack Nitzsche ("Memo from T" composed and performed by Mick Jagger
Cast: James Fox (Chas), Mick Jagger (Turner), Anita Pallenberg (Pherber), Michele Breton (Lucy), Stanley Meadows (Rosebloom), Allen Cuthbertson (lawyer), Anthony Morton (Dennis), Johnny Shannon (Harry), Anthony Valentine (Joey), Ann Sidney (Dana), John Bindon (Moody), John Sterland (chauffeur).
Running Time: 106 minutes
Premier: August 3, 1970, Trans-Lux East Theatre, New York
16mm. rental: Warner Brothers Non-Theatrical Division.

WALKABOUT (20th. Century-Fox, 1971)
Executive Producer: Max L. Raab
Producer: Si Litvinoff
Associate Producer: Anthony J. Hope
Assistant Director: Kevin Kavanagh
Screenplay: Edward Bond, from James Vance Marshall's novel *Walkabout* (1961)
Director of Photography: Nicholas Roeg
Designer: Brian Eatwell
Music: John Barry
Cast: Jenny Agutter (girl), Lucien John (brother), David Gumpilil (aborigine), John Meillon (father), Peter Carver (No Hoper), John Illingsworth (husband).
Running Time: 95 minutes

149

Rating: GP
Premiere: July 1, 1971, Plaza Theatre, New York
16mm. rental: Films, Inc.

DON'T LOOK NOW (an Anglo-Italian co-production by Casey Produc-
tions, London, and Eldorado Films, Rome, distributed by Paramount
Pictures, 1973)
Executive Producer: Anthony B. Unger
Producer: Peter Katz
Associate Producer: Frederico Mueller
Screenplay: Alan Scott and Chris Bryant, from Daphne du Maurier's
novelette *Don't Look Now* (1971)
Director of Photography: Anthony Richmond
Art Director: Giovanni Soccol
Set Designer: Francesca Chinanese
Music: Pino Donnagio
Sound: Rodney Holland
Editor: Graeme Clifford
Cast: Donald Sutherland (John Baxter), Julie Christie (Laura Baxter), Hilary
Mason (Heather), Clelia Matania (Wendy), Massimo Serato (Bishop
Barbarrigo), Renato Scarpa (Inspector Longhi).
Running Time: 110 minutes
Premiere: December 9, 1973, Sutton Theatre, New York
16mm. rental: Paramount

THE MAN WHO FELL TO EARTH (British Lion International, dis-
tributed by Cinema 5, 1976)
Executive Producer: Si Litvinoff
Producers: Michael Deeley and Barry Spikings
Associate Producer: John Peverall
Screenplay: Paul Mayersberg, from Walter Tevis's novel, *The Man Who
Fell to Earth* (1963).
Director of Photography: Anthony Richmond
Production Designer: Brian Eatwell
Music Director: John Phillips
Original Music: John Phillips
Sound: Stomo Yamashta
Editor: Graeme Clifford
Cast: David Bowie (Thomas Newton), Candy Clark (Mary Lou), Buck
Henry (Farnsworth), Rip Torn (Bryce).
Running Time: 158 minutes (uncut British version—American version runs
about 133 minutes)
Premiere: May 28, 1976, Cinema I and II, New York.
16mm. rental: Cinema 5

Index